Except For Nightmares

The True Story of Glenn Allen Carter

Merrie Miller

ISBN-10: 1463632231
ISBN-13: 9781463632236
Library of Congress Control Number: **XXXXX (If applicable)**
LCCN Imprint Name: **City and State (If applicable)**

CHAPTER 1

Regarding Glenn

What would it be like to have the eyes of God who has seen the past and looks far into the future? We could watch events evolve and shift together in the course of God's perfect plan and perhaps understand better why things happen the way they do. I can't see what God had in store for Glenn but I'm certain he gave me his story so I could heal.

I was just shy of ten in nineteen sixty-five when first presented with the news that Glenn had died. I remember that day because I was playing outside with a friend from across the street from me and looked up in time to see my Mother in the door way of our house looking intently in my direction. Now my mother was a meticulously tidy and organized woman who surely did not anticipate having a daughter who was the very antithesis of tidy and especially of organized. Needless to say, Mom was always very content when I was playing outside the house and didn't really go looking for me unless she was upset with me or there was some kind of emergency.

Watching Mom walk down those steps that day set all kinds of alarm bells off inside my head as I frantically tried to think about all the things I could have done to warrant her attention. In an instant I was out of the neighbour's yard and walking briskly to greet my Mother before she even crossed the street. This was a strategic move on my part not only to appease my Mother by showing her that I welcomed her attention (which I did not), but also to lessen the likelihood that my peers would have a bird's eye view of my mother dragging me inside our house by the lobe of my ear.

My mother was someone who did not try to hide her emotions, and I always knew what to look for when she was mad at me.   When she was mildly irritated her face was completely blank and her mouth was pursed a little. When she was really mad you could see pulsating jaw muscles, eyes that snapped and lips disappearing into a taught straight line. When I got to where she was standing in the yard I could see no indication of her being annoyed or enraged. Instead, she seemed a little reticent as she handed me a newspaper clipping and announced, "Your father died."

For a split second I panicked, but then I glanced down at the article and recognized that she meant Glenn and not the man who sat across from me that morning at the breakfast table reading his paper and sipping coffee. I remember looking up at Mom's face as she stood there watching me read the newspaper clipping and wondering what I should say about it. My Mother was a verbal economist and usually told us what she figured we ought to know and little else, so without any words; she took the clipping out of my hands then walked back into the house and put it somewhere in her closet where all the things she did not want us to get into were put. After that day, Mom stopped talking about Glenn as much. Occasionally she would come across something that reminded her of him and then she would say; "Your dad would have been a good man if it wasn't for that plate in his head."

Throughout the years my mother would periodically mention the plate in Glenn's head. The first mention came when I was too young to understand what she was talking about. As a consequence, I imagined the metal plate as some sort of evil animated dinnerware spinning around in Glenn's head and making him crazy. Mom, in her verbally economic way, didn't elaborate about how big the metal plate was, where exactly it was in Glenn's head or even what it looked like; so as I grew older and discounted the demonic dinnerware theory, I began to rationalize that it was some sort of large flat structure that was pressing down on Glenn's brain. This theory stuck with me until I received Glenn's service records and discovered that the metal plate was actually a small rectangular piece of tantalum covering up a hole in his skull.

That Glenn should have a piece of tantalum in his skull is quite ironic given the amount of misery he endured. I say this because of tantalum's origins from the Greek mythological son of Zeus, *Tantalus* who spent eternity up to his neck in water which flowed away from him when he tried to drink it and labored under a big rock that hung over his head and was poised to fall and crush him at any moment. It is a myth of great analogous possibilities concerning Glenn Allen Carter.

My Mother would not or could not elaborate effectively about Glenn's plate but would always refer to it as if it were the sole purveyor of all his irrational behaviour." Imagine my surprise when I discovered that the much-maligned metal plate had nothing to do with his downward spiral but was only a physical reminder of the carnage hiding invisibly behind.

I grew up fearing Glenn and part of it stemmed from Mom's anxiety about him, but another part came from the few memories I had of him and the terrible nightmares. Mom certainly was justified in her fear of Glenn, and she was right to warn us about him. What I did not necessarily need to know when I was six years old was how much Glenn disliked me and why she felt compelled to leave him for it. That Glenn should have a particular animus for me seemed to amplify my fear that Glenn could jump out from behind a bush at any moment and harm me. I know Mom did not mean to cause additional anxiety, but she was pretty young and did not associate my anxiety and nightmares with anything she was telling me.

It was always a heavy weight on me knowing that my own father, for some unknown reason, seemed to love Myra but not me. I didn't know his mind was damaged and he wasn't responsible for his actions, so I grew up thinking that something really must be wrong with me if my own Father didn't want me. After Glenn died, I heard little about him unless Myra or I asked a question of Mom or if she and Dad were having an argument and Mom got peeved enough to say, "You know, Glenn would have been a good man if it hadn't been for that plate in his head."

As the years passed and my night terrors and anxiety about Glenn started to subside; I started to entertain the idea that I might actually like to find out more about him and what was really behind his animosity toward me. I don't think Mom could ever say for sure why Glenn was aggressive toward me, but she did have a few theories. Her first theory was that Glenn didn't want any more children after Myra, and then she said he was fine with another child as long as it was a boy. The last theory she had about Glenn's attitude toward me was that he harbored a notion that Mom had been cheating on him and I was the bi-product of that. Mom's best friend also believed Glenn thought Mom was cheating on him, but said that he only believed that because he was impulsively chasing any pretty face that took his fancy and figured Mom was getting her own revenge by cheating too. Through research of my own, I have discovered that paranoia can be part and parcel with the sort of brain damage Glenn had.

It is a good thing that Glenn Allen Carter ceased to have access to our family, and a true blessing that Don Hanks entered our lives at such a critical stage. He became our father embraced Myra and I as if we had been born to him. Don Hanks was good natured, fun-loving and faithful, which Glenn could not be. The love and devotion our Dad showed us brought an enormous amount of healing and Mom made it clear from the start that we would never speak of Glenn in front of him because it would hurt his feelings. Of course Myra and I loved Dad with all our hearts and did not want to do anything to hurt his feelings so we would always make sure he wasn't around when we talked about Glenn or posed questions to Mom about him.

Of course, as Myra and I grew older, our curiosity about Glenn seemed to take on more urgency. It wasn't until I was nearly twenty years old that I finally drummed up enough courage to go and visit one of Glenn's brothers. Myra and I decided together that we would have that adventure. We could not travel far in my unreliable blue Datsun station-wagon so we chose to visit the brother that lived in Missoula Montana, which was only one hundred twenty-one miles from where we lived in Kalispell. Myra asked Mom to contact Gay Carter first to find out if it was alright to visit. After getting the O.K.; me, Myra and Myra's fiancé piled into my little blue car and made the journey to Missoula.

When we arrived at Gay's house, his wife, Dusty Carter, greeted us at the door and led us into the living room where her husband was sitting in his easy chair waiting for us. By my calculation, Gay was well into his fifties by then but looked more like thirty. He was shorter than I had imagined and had a muscular build with dark wavy hair and narrow blue eyes that seemed to look right through you. Unfortunately, I could tell right away as I walked into the living room that he did not approve of my short shorts; so I stood silently against the wall behind my sister and her fiancé during the entire visit. Gay didn't move from that easy chair the whole time we were there, but watched us stoically from the padded recesses of his chair and listened as Myra told him about what we were currently up to.

Unfortunately, neither Myra nor I could find the courage to ask Gay the one question that was foremost on our minds, namely; "What happened to Glenn that made him the way he was?" I just stood there feeling so anxious and uncomfortable the whole time that I started wishing I hadn't come in the first place. In retrospect, I think that being in the same room with Gay Carter felt uncomfortably close to being in the presence of Glenn himself.

After that brief awkward visit with Gay, I never really wanted to attempt another one. When Gay died in nineteen eighty-two, Mom took us to the reception after his burial so we could meet our other uncles who had travelled from Washington and California to attend his service. I was twenty-seven at the time and felt a lot less anxious about that meeting. Glenn's brother, Hugh, was there along with Brother Harry and Harry's son, Jimmy. Also present was Melville Somers, the husband of Glenn's sister, Thelma, who had passed away a year earlier. I remember that Harry and his son were smiling but Hugh and Skinny looked very sombre. Mom greeted them from a distance then Myra and I walked over and hugged each of the men and offered condolences, but again; few words were spoken. By the time I decided to write about Glenn, all those men were gone.

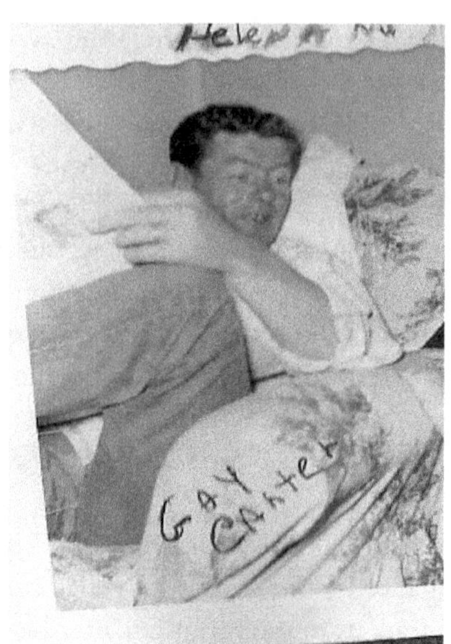

Gay Carter 1959

CHAPTER 2

Carter Family

Oh, the West Virginia hills! I must bid you now adieu.
In my home beyond the mountains I shall ever dream of you;
in the evening time of life, if my father only wills,
I shall still behold the vision of those West Virginia hills

From the state song Hills of West Virginia

When you're a child and someone hurts you, their essence weaves its way into your unconscious and lingers there until you have the strength and maturity to let it go. Glenn did that for me and my mother with all her anxiety about him inadvertently caused it to stay around for a very long time. That is primarily why it was so difficult for me to reach out to his brothers when I was a young adult. In the back of my mind they were Glenn by association, and Glenn was my bogyman. I regret that now because their information and perspectives would have been invaluable. The family members I did talk to after deciding to write about Glenn included Harry Carter's wife Rita, Thelma's daughter Karen, Hugh's wife, Janet, and two of Gay Carter's children.

At first I had some anxiety about talking to members of Glenn's family, but that dissipated quickly. They were honest, courageous and friendly people who spoke compassionately about a man who had caused irreparable damage to their families. Fortunately, mom had kept in touch with Rita and Karen and gay's children throughout years and had written all their addresses and phone numbers in her address book which she shared with me when I started thinking I might want to write Glenn's story. Thelma's daughter, Karen, was one of the first people I contacted.

I knew that Glenn had done something monstrous to Karen's family and that her parents had never forgiven him for it so I was relieved when Karen answered the phone and seemed pleasantly surprised that I had reached out to her. Karen told me that her mother had been the keeper of many family stories dating back before my grandparent's marriage. She also said that her mother had written her stories down and archived them with the Mormon Church many years ago, but when I tried to find them; they couldn't be found. It didn't really matter because Karen had already read her mother's journal and had memorized many of events over the years from her mother's retelling of them. She was more than happy to share them with me.

The name of Glenn's father was David Berry Carter and his mother's name was Minnie Pearl Rygsby. David was raised in a town called Trout Valley which is in Greenbrier County, West Virginia. Minnie was raised in a town called Glade, which was in Webster County, West Virginia. David's mother gave birth to David illegitimately and the severe scrutiny and prejudice about such a birth seemed to follow David like a dark cloud throughout his life. The name of David's natural father was John Carter.

David's mother married a man by the name of Gross when David was five and gave her son his last name. According to sources within the Carter family, David was treated severely by his stepfather and shortly before marrying Minnie, he changed his name back to the one written on his birth certificate, Carter.

Minnie's upbringing was starkly different than that of David's. Minnie was the seventh of eight children. Her mother had passed away when she was small and her father, a Baptist minister, never remarried. Minnie was nurtured and raised by the older siblings in her family who doted on her and her little sister. Minnie was not treated severely like David but was watched over and cared for tenderly.

Minnie and David were introduced through two of Minnie's brothers who worked with David on West Virginia's C&O railroad. According to Karen, David was smitten with the beautiful young woman with the dark curly hair and brilliant blue eyes the minute he laid eyes on her, but Minnie had ideas of her own. Karen said Minnie was in love with a boy in Washington State that she had met while visiting her oldest brother and his family, but kept it a secret from her brothers in West Virginia. Karen said this caused some consternation because David assumed Minnie was going to marry him and made that assumption plain to her two brothers who in turn began to pressure Minnie to accept David's proposal.

Minnie told Thelma that she did not want to marry David initially and was alarmed by her brothers' insistence, so she fled to Brush Prairie, Washington to be near the young man she favored. Unfortunately for young Minnie, her impulsive decision created a firestorm of sorts that divided her family. The two brothers in West Virginia threatened to disown her when they discovered what she had done and eventually convinced the oldest brother in Washington State to take their side.

Karen said losing the affections of her brothers was a non-starter for Minnie so she agreed to marry David Carter. David then traveled to Washington where he and Minnie were married in her Brother's home. Afterwards, they traveled back to West Virginia and settled down in Sutton.

After settling in, Minnie and David immediately started adding to their family. Minnie gave birth to Thelma in nineteen hundred and eighteen and then had Gay a year later. Five years after that, in nineteen twenty-four, they had another son that they named Hubert (Hugh).

When Hugh was still a toddler, David was ran afoul of a high-ranking member of the KKK who accused him of bothering one of his female family members. Shortly after that revelation, the family left West Virginia. It's not perfectly clear why David Chose Missoula, but I suspect it had something to do with the railroad because of his work as a mechanic for the C&O. Minnie and David continued to add to their family after their move with the birth of Harry Carter in nineteen twenty-eight and then Glenn a year and a half later in August of nineteen thirty.

David and Minnie were definitely southern rural folk, but did not exactly fit the Hillbilly stereotype of people raised in the hills and hollers of West Virginia. That said, their rural humble beginnings made their transition from Sutton to Missoula a little startling. When David and Minnie left West Virginia,the abundant timber and railroad jobs that were available around the turn of the century were all but gone. Missoula, on the other hand, had a thriving lumber industry, an expansive and busy railroad yard and even an institute of higher learning. Missoula's population at the time was fourteen times as much as Sutton's. Of course, along with a larger population came all the small businesses that kept that population entertained like honky-tonks and houses of ill repute which were not as prevalent where they hailed from, and certainly not to Minnie's liking.

According to Gay's daughter, Nancy; Thelma and her father had the most difficulty adapting to their new surroundings. Nancy said Gay and Thelma's first day at Lowell Elementary School was particularly humiliating because they arrived shoeless just like they might have had it been a rural West Virginia school house. The fact that they had no shoes on and spoke with a thick southern twang gave everyone the impression that they'd just fallen off the turnip truck and kids started harassing them and calling them dirty hillbillies. Nancy said those same kids would also wait for her father and aunt after school every day, pepper them with insults then chase them all the way the home with sticks.

Minnie bought shoes for the pair right away after she realized what was going on, but it didn't affect the attitude of the children who kept right on pestering Gay and Thelma. According to Nancy, Gay and Thelma began to get real tired of being chased home every day and decided to take a stand and give their pursuers a demonstration of the rock throwing skills they had honed on the squirrels and cowbirds of West Virginia. After a few well place thumps on the noggins, the bullies learned not to mess with them. Nancy said Thelma and Gay earned a great deal of respect for sticking up for themselves that way.

Once Thelma and Gay understood what it took to keep the wolves at bay, they began to move up in the pack and eventually reached the top of the pecking order. While they were cementing their reputations, the younger brothers were watching from the wings and listening with interest to the stories Gay and Thelma told about what it took to get some respect at Lowell Elementary School. By the time Glenn was ready for primary school, the Carter name was well known and respected. So he did no experience near as much trouble like his older siblings had.

After their move to Missoula, David Carter did indeed get hired on by the Northern Pacific Railway as a mechanic. When the depression hit, he was laid off from that job and forced to take a employment with the WPA which sometimes meant travelling away from home for long periods of time. Karen told me that David was away from home quite a lot during his children's formative years either working or attempting to find work while Minnie did her best to manage her high spirited children.

In spite of her best efforts, Karen said Minnie had a heck of a time managing Harry when David was away but when David was at home; the children were less likely to misbehave. David was a quiet stern man, and I got the impression from speaking to family members that David not only demanded obedience from his children, he expected them to be highly independent and solve their own problems. The Carter children were not known to argue with David, but Minnie's bark was less audible and her bite lest painful unless she really had her dander up.

Karen said that Minnie seemed to have a particularly hard time keeping Harry from running into downtown Missoula when he was very young. So great was her frustration with her willful young son that her only recourse was to strip him down to his underwear, put one of Thelma's old dresses on him then tie a rope harness around him and tie the other end to the rope around the birch tree in their front yard. Karen said Harry's brothers teased him mercilessly about that and Harry just yelled and bawled and tried his best to get free, which he eventually did.

Minnie mustn't have tied her knots tight enough on the legendary day Harry Carter managed to free himself from his tethers, dispense with the dress and head into town in his boxers and T-shirt. Minnie later found out that Harry was seen in town near the brothels begging for pennies from the ladies who lived there so he could buy candy. Karen said that a few hours after Harry's escape, a fancy car pulled up in front of the Carter household and a prostitute with a couple bags full of groceries in her arms stepped out followed by Harry. Harry was just trying to get a few pennies from the woman and had told her that his family was starving. Of course the woman believed the small scantily clad child and instead of giving him pennies, she bought groceries for his family instead.

Karen said that Minnie was mortified to see Harry in his underwear and even more mortified that a prostitute was offering her charity. Minnie declined the woman's offer according to Karen then got Harry by the ear and marched him into the house with a lilac switch.

According to family sources, and Glenn himself; he didn't get into as much trouble as Harry did when he was a small child. In clinical notes from his services records, Glenn stated that he was sickly most of his childhood and nearly perished from influenza as an infant. He also stated that he had Rheumatic Fever that kept him out of school for several months around the age of ten. In those same clinical notes, Glenn gives a glimpse of his relationship with his parents. He stated that because of being sickly, he and his mother spent a lot of time together and became very close. Glenn also stated, resentfully, that he believed Minnie wanted him to be more like a girl, and because of that; David did not want to do things with him like he did with his older brothers.

Inferences in Glenn's clinical notes and comments from family members paint a portrait of a Minnie Carter who was not pleased with how the older boys behaved and decided that Glenn was going to be her project. Glenn stated in his clinical notes that Minnie's plan worked pretty well when he was little because he did not buck the system or try to escape like Harry did. For the most part he said he did almost everything his mother told him to do and even obeyed his teachers religiously when he first started going to Lowell Elementary.

Unfortunately all that good behavior resulted in some misery for Glenn when his older brothers and their pals began harassing him and calling him a mama's boy and teacher's pet. By the time Glenn reached his middle grades he had fallen in line behind his brothers. He might have been the darling of Lowell Elementary School in his early years, but as he states in his clinical records;"It didn't last very long."

By the time Glenn entered middle school, all of Minnie's efforts to make a little gentleman out of him fell by the wayside as he started aping his brothers and their roughshod ways. According to his testimony in clinical notes, Glenn's academic career ended in his first year of high school when the principal confiscated a pistol and half empty bottle of whisky from his locker.

Glenn bonded very closely to his brothers and would always try to tag along and get in on whatever they had up their sleeves. He figured they'd always be there for him, but when he was eleven years old that all changed. That was the year Pearl Harbor was bombed and a tsunami of patriotism swept over the nation. Every able bodied man was tripping over themselves to be the first in line at the recruiting stations and twenty-three-year-old Gay and his eighteen-year-old brother Hugh were no exception.

The two oldest Carter brothers enlisted in the Navy and were off to California for basic training within a month. Then in nineteen forty-four, David and Minnie gave their written permission for Harry to join the Merchant Marines leaving Glenn all alone without the company of his brothers for the very first time in his life. Glenn did try and get in on the action like his brothers according to his military records. He was four months shy of his seventeenth birthday when he attempted to enlist in the Navy but was sent home before getting to basic training. According to family sources, Glenn was not only lost without his brothers, he was very upset about not being able to show that he was patriotic as well.

After his brothers left, Glenn stated in his clinical records that he joined a gang of boys with delinquent interests. Soon after he started running with these boys, he began to get into some serious trouble. I got the impression that getting into trouble in the Carter family was acceptable only if you could get out of it by yourself and not make the folks open their pocketbook. Unfortunately, Glenn violated that rule when he and members of his gang stole an expensive piece of farm equipment. As a result of that larceny, David and Minnie were forced to use their savings to hire an attorney and keep their youngest son out of jail. Minnie and David were very upset with Glenn but that apparently didn't concern him near as much as the thought of his brothers finding out and beating the tar out of him.

During the time Glenn and his gang were getting into trouble, Thelma and her family moved back to Missoula and his sister didn't have any reservations about giving Glenn an earful concerning his bad behavior. Thelma and Glenn had always been very close, almost as close as he and Minnie had been. Thelma was thirteen when Glenn was born and was there helping her mother doctor him through his illnesses and spoiling him rotten.

Thelma Married Melville Sommers in nineteen thirty-six when Glenn was just five years old. Melville didn't keep his name very long after marrying Thelma because Gay thought the name was questionable and gave him a new one, "Skinny." It was a bit of irony on Gay's part because Melville wasn't skinny at all but it stuck and pretty soon nobody even remembered his real name except maybe Skinny himself.

In the fall of nineteen thirty-six, Skinny and Thelma had their first child and named him Gene. Growing up, Gene and Glenn were close enough in age that they acted more like brothers when they were together. Much to Thelma and Skinny's chagrin, Gene started talking and acting like he was a Carter brother mini-me. Skinny was especially unimpressed with Glenn's influence on his young son. Just as the war was ending, Thelma and Skinny moved to Alaska. I got the feeling that their move was primarily one of financial opportunity but partially prompted by their concern for Gene and the influence Thelma's brothers had over him, especially her youngest brother, Glenn.

By his own testimony, Glenn did misbehave and get into some trouble while his brothers were gone, but his behavior was not that far removed from the behavior he'd seen in two of his older brothers when they lived at home. My mother always referred to the Carter boys as "rounders", and if I were to make an assessment; I would say that a little Ritalin in their drinking water might have calmed things down a bit in the Carter household.

Hugh Carter was not overtly rambunctious like his three brothers according to family members. Glenn described Hugh in his clinical notes as being quiet like their dad and less likely to get into trouble. My Mother said Hugh backed his brothers up when they needed it, but enjoyed the ladies a lot more than he enjoyed drinking and fighting.

Nancy Carter said that there was always an unspoken agreement between brothers and sister that whenever one of them was in trouble the others would come running, even Hugh. It was a righteous familial bond that would greatly test their mettle after Glenn came home from Letterman Hospital.

Glenn in 1947, seventeen years old

FAMILY HISTORY: The patient's family came from a medium sized
town in Montana and besides the living parents, includes 3 older
brothers and one older sister. Financially, the family is average,
although during the depression, the father had to work on the WPA
and was not too well off. At present, he is a mechanic for a
railroad line. The father never liked to do anything with the
patient, and the patient thinks that he doesn't care much for him.
Patient was the closest to his mother because he was the baby of
the family - she always treated the patient "like a baby" which
she never liked. The mother is very affectionate to the patient,
but he feels she has always tried to tell him what to do. Patient
states that he has always been wild, has always gotten into
fights, got into trouble with the police, just like two of his
older brothers "the roughest guys in town". He said that he used
to look up to them and tried to ape them. The third brother is in
the Navy and is very quiet like the father, never drinking or
getting into fights. The sister is married at present and lives
in Alaska.

Excerpt from Glenn's clinical notes talking about
family

CHAPTER 3

Glenn, Fort Ord 1950

In The Army

And God said to David "You are not to build a house for my Name, because you have shed much blood on the earth in my sight."

In nineteen seventy-three, eighty percent of all the service records of Army personnel who served our country between November 1, nineteen-twelve and January 1, nineteen-sixty were lost from the National Personnel Records Center (NPRC) in St. Louis, Missouri due to a massive fire.

I wasn't aware of the fire before I sent a request for Glenn's military records and only found out about it by reading some of the comments from family members of service men posted on the Chosin Few web site. They talked about their desperate search for information about family members after learning that the massive fire at the NPRC had destroyed any trace of their service in Korea.

I became discouraged after learning about the fire and lowered my expectations of ever receiving Glenn's records. Imagine my surprise and joy when after eight months, the Army finally came through and sent me Glenn's complete military record. Those sixty-eight pages of copied military typeface were more precious than gold as far as I was concerned because they defied the odds and gave me the answers about Glenn I'd been searching for.

After Glenn's records arrived in the mail, I immediately started scanning the pages for information. At first, I wondered whether I would be able to decipher enough of it to understand what he went through because the old typeface in his records was sometimes faded and blurred. I spent weeks reading and re-reading his records, sometimes with a magnifying glass trying to accurately decipher words by looking at each letter individually and filling in the broken pieces. I was eventually able to decipher it all and construct a time line of events including the battles his company fought through in Korea, the exact day of his injury and his year and a half odyssey at Letterman Hospital.

The first page of Glenn's records revealed that Glenn was nineteen years eight months of age when inducted into the Army at a recruiting station in Butte, Montana. After applying his signature to the necessary paperwork and taking a physical, he was bussed to Fort Ord on California's Monterey Bay for basic training.

Chart notes penned by an army psychiatrist who had an initial interview with Glenn prior to being discharged from the service state that Glenn finished his basic training without incident. To me this suggests that Glenn performed much better in a highly structured environment like the Army as compared to running buck wild in and around Missoula Montana.

According to military records, Glenn's regiment left Fort Ord for a tent city in Japan on the lower slopes of Mt. Fujiyama to join other troops from the seventh division. While Glenn's division trained at Camp Fujiyama, high command made a decision to integrate nearly eight thousand Republic of Korea soldiers into their ranks. They did so because they had already sent an inordinate number of troops to the Koran peninsula beforehand which left the rest of the division woefully under strength. Because of that integration, each soldier in Glenn's division was paired with a South Korean partner for training and combat. I can only assume that Glenn had a South Korean buddy because there was no mention of it in his records or accounts from family members.

By reading the information in Glenn's military records and researching information about the Korean War, I was able to chart the movements of Glenn's regiment and company up until the day of his injury. What I discovered was that Glenn and his regiment embarked on troop transports and landed at Inchon Harbour in South Korea on September 15, nineteen-fifty. Glenn and his company would have been among the first to reach the Yalu River, the geographical border between Communist China and Korea. Shortly after that event, the Seventh division became part of a three thousand-man U.S. Army task force called Regimental Combat Team (RCT) Thirty-One. The seventh division then joined with the first Marine Division under the umbrella of X-Corps commanded by Major General Ned Almond.

According to historical accounts, Ned Almond's first command came during WWII when he was assigned to the ninety second infantry division from nineteen forty-two to nineteen forty-five. Apparently General Marshall believed Almond would excel at the assignment he was given, but the division suffered from low morale and performed poorly in combat. According to those same historical accounts, Almond did not take responsibility for his troop's performance, but rather blamed it on the fact that it was comprised almost exclusively of African-American soldiers whom he considered inferior. Almond went on to advise the Army against ever using African-Americans in combat again.

After assuming command in Korea, I read that Almond faced resistance again. This time it was from marines who questioned his tactical prowess. They believed that he did not always make good strategic decisions that would keep them from losing more of their troops than was necessary. Marine General Oliver Smith actually disobeyed a direct order from Almond by refusing to let him direct the formation of marine troops around Chosin Reservoir in the same way he had directed the army. Accounts from military historians state that General Smith's actions insured that his troops fared much better than their Army counterparts who were widely dispersed around Chosin Reservoir.

General Almond was also described in some first-hand accounts as detached and unable to relate to the common soldier. I read that when he went to the front and visited troops, he did so in a trailer equipped with an alfresco shower. The Soldiers in the trenches he was inspecting did not have the luxury of showering daily nor adequate shelter against the harsh Korean winter. Most slept upright in foxholes lined with sleeping bags, trying to insulate themselves as best they could against the blistering cold. It was in sharp contrast to the

accommodations General Almond enjoyed. An account given
by one of General Almond's aides describes how Almond was
conducting an inspection of some of those soldiers one
afternoon and mentioned how cold it must have been the night
before because of a thin film of ice he found on his nightstand.
The aide said a lone anonymous voice shot back, "That's really
too @#$%&!* bad sir. Some military historians state that
Almond considered himself above reproach because of his close
relationship with General MacArthur. I don't know if that is
true, but what is historically correct is that when Lieutenant
General Ridgeway took over after Truman relieved MacArthur;
Almond's command was severely reduced.

Rodney Brewer, Military.com
The Korean War: The Chinese Intervention, pp 27–28

CHAPTER 4

Glenn's service with company B, 31st infantry

Baker Company

If any question why we died, tell them, because our fathers lied.
Rudyard Kipling

Captain Charles Peckham was Glenn's company commander. He commanded B (Baker) Company and unlike General Almond, was held in high regard by his troops. I learned that Glenn and the rest of B Company were engaged in a battle with North Koreans a day before his twentieth birthday on August 13, nineteen-fifty. Unfortunately, they lost that battle as North Koreans greatly outnumbered them and his company had to retreat. I also learned that on November 29, all of Baker Company was pulled into a taskforce to fight alongside the British Commonwealth Brigade (BCB), commanded by Captain Douglas Drysdale.

I don't presume to be a military historian, but after reading accounts of some of the troops who survived the Korean War; it seems to me that Marine's voices were very loud but the Army's voice was missing. Almost all of the accounts that made their way into Hollywood movies and history books came from marines who didn't seem to trust the Army's high command and inadvertently or not, seemed to dismiss the Army's contributions to the war effort. That is probably why there wasn't as much public recognition for the brave soldiers of the seventh infantry and their sacrifices. So many of the battles fought by the marines were glorified for all posterity by the movie industry in the nineteen fifties and sixties but I don't know of one major battle featuring the sacrifices of the Army that was ever considered for production.

Before receiving Glenn's records in the mail, I hadn't really given a lot of thought about the Korean War and didn't understand how terrible it truly was, particularly for the seventh division. After researching it from different perspectives, I'm reasonably sure that the Korean War was fought over idealistic political views rather than an imminent threat to the security of nations. What I am certain of is that Glenn's Baker Company and all its counterparts fought bravely and were sacrificed for their efforts.

Like many of the ground troops in the Korean War, Glenn's company had to advance over rugged mountainous terrain while trying to survive the bitter extremes of the Korean winter. The seventh army was particularly impacted because the chain of command failed to adequately outfit many its soldiers well enough to survive the harsh Korean winters. Consequently, way too many men died from hypothermia rather than wounds incurred in combat.   Their Marine counterparts were much better equipped to face the harsh winters and often referred to their Army counterparts as "poor sons of dogs (or something like that)" when they observed how ill-equipped some troops were for such extreme conditions.

After the dust settled, historians sometimes compared the missteps of high command in the Korean War to those of another infamous army general who perished at the Battle of Little Bighorn in eighteen seventy-six. The eerie parallels between what transpired at the Battle of the Little Big Horn and what happened in Korea couldn't be more pronounced. Custer discounted the natives just as historians say MacArthur did the Chinese. It is evidenced by the way both Custer and MacArthur seemed so certain of victory that they rejected counsel from their officers on the ground and orchestrated an attack without a thorough investigation into the position and numbers of the enemy. If they had investigated, they would have realized that there was quite a large group of enemy combatants positioning themselves tactically to respond to their advances. Historical accounts also state that both Custer and MacArthur thought so little of the potential of their enemies that they spread their troops out in a disastrously similar manner making them even more vulnerable to the attack that ensued.

The assault on Custer and his troops was one the greatest fiascos of the U.S. Army. As Custer led the charge on an Indian village, thousands of Lakota, Cheyenne, and Arapaho warriors charged down from the hills catching him and his men completely by surprise. They forced Custer's unit back onto a dusty ridge parallel to the Little Bighorn River, surrounded them and then killed all two hundred sixty eight men including Custer himself. Seventy three years later, General MacArthur declares that the Korean Conflict was over and that their mission to push back the communists was a success while hundreds of thousands of Chinese soldiers silently crossed the Yalu River (just like Lakota braves crossing the Little Big Horn) and attacked UN troops. The date was November 6, nineteen-fifty when MacArthur's Far Eastern command listed the total number of Chinese troops active in combat as thirty-four thousand when in reality; over three-hundred thousand CCF soldiers organized into thirty divisions had already moved into Korea and were engaged in battle.

On October 27, nineteen-fifty, General Almond ordered the elements of RTC Thirty-one to spread their troops out around Chosin Reservoir some two-hundred fifty miles apart from each other much like Custer did when he divided his seventh Calvary soldiers into three groups to make sure no Indian braves escaped. By spreading them out, MacArthur isolated the troops who had no idea that two reinforced Chinese Divisions (over seventeen thousand Peoples Liberation Army soldiers) had surrounded them just like the Dakota braves who surrounded Custer and his men. I wonder if Major General Almond or General MacArthur thought about their predecessor as events unfolded in Korea. The sad truth, according to many military experts, is that a lot of the casualties that came out of the Korean War might have been prevented had high command learned something from the tragic missteps of George Armstrong Custer.

General George Armstrong
Custer

General Ned Almond

CHAPTER 5

Hell's Fire valley

Here dead we lie
because we did not choose
to live and shame the land
from which we sprung.

AE Housman

According to first-hand accounts, Glenn's commander, Captain Charles Peckham and the rest of Baker Company had been on special detail and were nearing Koto-ri in route north to re-join the Marine's First Battalion when Peckham received orders from Marine Commanders General O.P. Smith and Cornel Lewis (Chesty) Puller to lead an organized special column setting up in Koto-ri.   Sometime later, marine commanders named that special column <u>Task Force Drysdale</u> in deference to the British Commander who was first at Koto-ri.

On the morning of November 29, nineteen-fifty; accounts state that Major General O. P. Smith ordered Chesty Puller to send a task force to "run the gauntlet" and open up the road between Koto-ri and Hagaru-ri so that his marines could get the reinforcements they needed to keep their stronghold. The taskforce that was assembled consisted of Drysdale's Forty-first Royal Commandos, Captain Carl Sitter's G Company, Third Battalion First Marines, Peckham's Baker CompanyThirty-first Infantry Regiment and various headquarters and services Marines. In total, I read that the task force consisted of about eleven hundred men and one-hundred forty vehicles.

When the task force started out, written accounts state that Peckham and B Company were in front of the column and Peckham was moving his men forward with great care while drawing the Chinese down from the heights. Behind Baker Company, Marine Captain Carl Sitter's George Company fought off the Chinese infantrymen driven briefly to ground by Peckham's company. While Baker Company was inching forward in the column lead, reports state that Colonel Drysdale became impatient with the pace. There was some speculation that Colonel Drysdale felt that he was not obliged to consult with Captain Peckham in spite of the fact that Chesty Puller had personally spoke to Peckham about commanding the lead of the column.

According to written testimony, it was well past noon and Captain Peckham was directing the loading of the lead platoon's trucks following the reduction of yet another roadside stronghold when a tank surged past him. The next vehicle was a jeep bearing Drysdale, who yelled above the din, "Let's move forward!' Witnesses state that Peckham demurred because he had wounded men on his hands and felt they should not advance until they were out of the fray. Colonel Drysdale then shouted "Tally Ho!' and took off with forty-one Commando, all the tanks and Captain Sitter's George Company in tow. The Chinese immediately spotted Drysdale's advance and bombarded his entourage with mortars and rapid gun fire to disable the tanks and pick off the troops riding in the back of transport trucks. As a result, a massive traffic jam ensued and the convoy with Drysdale in the lead became fragmented.

Sources indicate that Peckham initially tried to navigate through the smoldering mess created by the hasty advance, but could not. He also could not move back in the column due to heavy enemy resistance. Unable to proceed, Peckham deployed his troops in roadside ditches to return the Chinese fire from the heights. Meanwhile, after receiving a reinforcement of tanks, General Smith told Drysdale to press on at all costs." Drysdale, responded, "Very well then, we'll give them a show," and passed the word that they were going to run the gauntlet to Hagaru-ri. Later that evening, Drysdale and his entourage arrived in Hagaru-ri with a slightly wounded Drysdale entering the division command post to announce proudly, "Forty-First Commando present for duty."

Colonel Drysdale made it to his destination in relatively good shape but those four hundred men he left behind without radio contact and surrounded by CCF soldiers were doomed. Hell's Fire Valley was an appropriate moniker for the area where trapped members of the task force battled for their lives. Some accounts state that Drysdale assumed that Peckham and the rest of the column were behind him and did not realize that they were still trapped there, but that doesn't seem to be the account of events from those few who survived the ordeal.

The troops left behind were composed of about sixty Royal Marines, all of B Company Thirty-First Infantry Regiment, Heavy weapons D Company and the assorted headquarters and services Marines. There were four pockets of troops under siege and strung out along roughly two-thirds of a mile. Many of those men perished in battle and others froze to death or became POWs. Peckham eventually negotiated surrender to the enemy rather than lose his whole company.

There were some soldiers able to make it back through the column to Koto-ri, and according to sources; those were mainly the South Korean draftees who started running once the fighting started. Of the eleven hundred men assigned to Task Force Drysdale, approximately three hundred arrived at Hagaru-ri, five hundred were killed or wounded, 135 were taken prisoner and the rest (mainly South Koreans), made it back to Koto-ri. Also destroyed were seventy-five vehicles out of one hundred and forty-one that began the march. In spite of all that, Chesty Puller seemed to justify the human cost by stating it was a successful campaign because it brought reinforcements to his marines under siege at Hagaru-ri.

Glenn was twenty years and three months of age when he entered Hell's Fire Valley. Through communication with the "Chosin Few" military organization, I spoke to a man who stated he was beside a young soldier who took a bullet through his helmet and looked very much like the picture I had posted of my father on the Chosin Few website. The man, Jack Chapman, was part of the Army's Heavy Weapons Platoon and said that they were all standing in a truck with their heads tucked in their jacket flaps trying to soften the effect of the blistering cold when small arms fire from the heights started to pick off some of the men. Mr. Chapman said a bullet found its way through the young man's helmet and he figured it had travelled all the way through his head. Mr. Chapman then said that he and another soldier took the young man out of the truck and laid him beside the road for the medics (who were farther back in the column), to attend to. Mr. Chapman said he and the other man climbed back into the truck and before long, the sniping became more intense and machine guns began spraying bullets. Mr. Chapman was shot six times, then captured by the Chinese and spent thirty-three months in POW camps. The date was November 30, nineteen-fifty. According to Glenn's military records, the bullet that wounded him had gone through his helmet but not all the way through his head. Glenn told medical personnel that he was unconscious for a short time and when he regained consciousness, two Chinese soldiers took him into custody. Glenn said he struggled to get free of his captors and was struck by a rifle butt and taken to a holding area with other POWs.

Glenn told family members that the Chinese forced him and the rest of the POWs to march two or three miles at night to get to another holding area. In his records he describes an incident during that march that disturbed him quite a lot. He said he was standing next to a buddy when a Chinese guard put the barrel of his rifle next to the man's head and shot him dead for the simple act of lighting a cigarette.

Shortly after dawn of the next day, Glenn's Chinese captors stopped at another holding station and it was there that he says a buddy overpowered a Chinese guard and helped him and at least five other soldiers escape. Glenn told his brothers that he didn't think he would have survived very long if that soldier had not helped him escape because his mind was fogging up and he was slowing down. Because of his un-named buddy's efforts, Glenn was able to get to the evacuation hospital in Yong Dong Po and receive triage for his wound.

After the battle of Hell's Fire Valley had subsided, the commandos of the rear guard came into the valley and were quoted as saying, "Coming back through the area was almost as bad as fighting north through it." They described dead frozen soldiers in gruesome postures buried under mounds of snow and perfectly preserved where they had fallen. They also described how the trucks and jeeps from Drysdale's entourage were bumper to bumper and all were either burned or shot to pieces and were still smouldering. The battle of Hell's Fire Valley has been described as the greatest battle Hollywood forgot.

Eric Hammel History Magazine

http://www.kmike.com/CombatActions/Chosin.htm

Birchard Lee (Bert) KortegaardThe coldest winter: America and the Korean War by David Halberstam

Korean War; ***http://www.korean-war.com/****Information compiled by Ed Eva*

http://www.historynet.com/korean-war-death-of-task

Combating Cold Korea

Karl Warner, U. S. Army Heritage and Education Center

CHAPTER 6

Pvt. Carter Is Wounded, Captured and Returned

Private Glenn Carter, 20, 1438 Phillips street, who was wounded and captured by communist forces in the battle for North Korean water reservoirs, November 30, has been returned to the American force, his family has been informed.

Private Carter, who is the son of Mr. and Mrs. Dave B. Carter of Missoula, is now in Tokyo, Japan. He joined the army in the early part of April and has been in the far east since the first of September. Private Carter was employed by the American Crystal Sugar company while living in Missoula.

Article from The Missoulian News paper
1951

Initial Care

Every night I lie awake
And every day I lie abed
And hear the doctors, Pain and Death,
Conferring at my head.

Sara Teasdale

Glenn didn't stay long at the evacuation hospital at Yong Dong Po but was transported to the Army's sixty-fourth field hospital in Japan where doctors examined his head wound and removed a twenty-five calibre armour-piercing bullet embedded in bone at about the midline of his skull. They then made an incision in the protective outside covering of the brain called the Dura Mater and removed two small blood clots and tiny pieces of bone from the cortex of his brain. The surgeons didn't replace the shattered area of Glenn's skull but seemed to know that allowing room for the brain to swell would benefit Glenn in the long run.

In Glenn's military records, they called the opening in his skull a bony defect. The bullet that hit Glenn's head didn't penetrate the Dura but the force of the bullet hitting his head propelled tiny fragments of bone through the Dura mater into the Cerebral Cortex, and the concussion of the bullet hitting his skull produced the blood clots. Chart notes indicate that the surgeon described the frontal lobes of his cerebral cortex as being soft, particularly the right frontal lobe.

As soon as Glenn was stable, they evacuated him to Kelly Air force Base in Texas where he transferred planes and flew to Letterman Army Hospital on San Francisco's Presidio. The records generated at Letterman comprised the bulk of Glenn's military record and provided details about his combat service, his previous history in Montana and a precise timetable of his physical and mental deterioration. Harry's wife, Rita, told me that she and Harry went to visit Glenn after his arrival at Letterman, and the bullet that had been extracted from his head was taped to the collar of his hospital gown. She said he was very happy to see them and was pretty drowsy but able to talk a little. Glenn's parents also travelled to California to see Glenn around the same time.

The first thing medical personnel at Letterman did was compile a pertinent medical history on Glenn. It included his medical history before his service as well as his injury in Korea. The physician from Letterman who gave Glenn his initial examination and looked over his medical history wrote in summary that there was no present neurological residue, meaning that Glenn wasn't experiencing any seizures at that time.

     Glenn had a complete physical on January 5, nineteen fifty-one. The physician who performed that more comprehensive physical listened to and felt around for all the important organs, checked Glenn's reflexes from head to toe, and poked around in every orifice and cavity. The doctor even drew a stick figure with an "x" on the many parts of its body they tested for nerve conductivity. The physician then carefully massaged the area of the bony defect in Glenn's skull and wrote that it had healed quite well and had a pulse. In his summary notes, the physician wrote, "There are no complaints from the patient at present, except for nightmares."

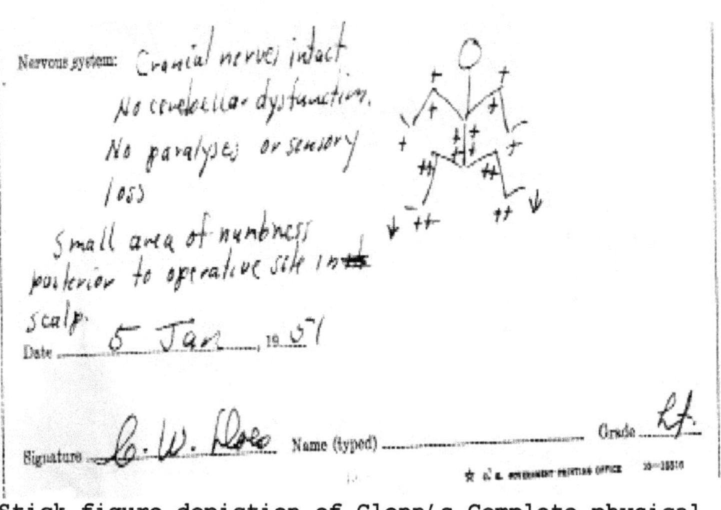

Stick figure depiction of Glenn's Complete physical
01-05-1951

As a result a bifrontal craniectomy was
performed through a horshoe type of flap
& a comminuted depressed fracture of the
right frontal bone removed. Bullet had
penetrated the bone, but not the dura.
A small epidural hematoma & subdural hematoma
were removed. The bullet was also removed.
Softening of the right frontal lobe was present.
Wound closed uneventfully & patient has
made rapid recovery. without neurological
defect.

No complaints at present, except for
nightmares.

Except for Nightmares

CHAPTER 7

Letterman Army Hospital that Glenn knew

Letterman Hospital wwith President Mckinley

Letterman Army Hospital

I have a dream—a dreadful dream—
A dream that is never done,
I watch a man go out of his mind,
And he is My Mother's Son.

Rudyard Kipling

Letterman Hospital was once located on the historic Presidio of San Francisco. The Presidio has been a fortified location since seventeen seventy-six when the Spanish made it the military centre of their expansion in the area. Spain bequeathed the Presidio to Mexico, which in turn relinquished it to the United States in eighteen forty-seven. The military hospital on the Presidio was established in eighteen ninety-eight but it wasn't until nineteen hundred and eleven that they named it after Major Jonathan Letterman who was the medical director of the Army of the Potomac and a founding father of military medicine.

In nineteen hundred and one, Letterman hospital was the first Army general hospital to employ women of the Army Nurse Corps. The only time civilians were admitted to the hospital was after the earthquake and fire of nineteen hundred and six. During that time medical officers from the Presidio took care of sanitation in the refugee camps that sprung up over night in city parks and on the Presidio. In the early part of the twentieth century, Letterman Hospital was the Army's largest general hospital. Many of the original buildings were still in use when Glenn arrived at Letterman Hospital in nineteen fifty-one.

On January 10, nineteen fifty-one, right after Glenn

first arrived at Letterman; an x-ray was taken of his head. In spite of spotting a pinpoint piece of metal left behind in the soft tissue of his brain; they said they observed nothing abnormal in major brain processes and described his brain as normal in size and position. Around that same time, Glenn was given his first in a series of electroencephalograms (EEGs) and the interpretation of that EEG was that there was slightly abnormal electrical activity in the right side of his brain. It was a common reading for a head wound, and the EEG was of little concern to the neurologist who reviewed it. Because of this initial assessment of Glenn, Lt. Col. Greenwood wrote in Glenn's clinical progress notes that he believed the injury to Glenn's head was not debilitating. Greenwood went on to state that he thought Glenn was well enough to return to duty after a furlough. That was exactly nine days after Glenn arrived at the facility.

On January 24, just twelve days after Greenwood's assessment and before Glenn left for furlough; he fell to the floor near his hospital bed and struck his forehead on a chair. According to his records, Glenn was having a seizure in which "All four extremities shook in tonic motion and his mouth frothed." It was Glenn's first seizure after his head injury and it raised a red flag for the physicians who originally indicated there was no residue.

In progress notes dated January 25, Lt. Javar wrote that Glenn had been alert and asymptomatic since his single seizure and noted that he was under careful observation and started receiving one and one-half grains of Dilantin and one-half grain of Phenobarbital. These same progress notes included a full acknowledgment by Lt. Col. Greenwood of the onset of neurological residue (seizures) which was absent in his wound history. The colonel went on to recommend that "PFC Carter remain on anticonvulsant medication for a year and go back on duty in about forty days if there was evidence that the seizures could be controlled by medications."

In nineteen fifty-one, Dilantin was the go-to drug designed specifically to alleviate erratic electrical activity in the brain that caused seizures. Studies have shown that seizures alone can shorten a life and can contribute to brain damage. A serious side effect of Dilantin, however, is the propensity for suicidal thoughts and tendencies in the patient as well as psychosis and locomotor dysfunction. Phenobarbital is known to cause hyperactivity, behavioural problems and even dementia.

Having that bony defect in his head also made Glenn's brain more vulnerable to injury much like the soft spot on a baby's skull. After Glenn returned from leave on March 7th, he stated that he had received an injury to his head but did not indicate how it happened. Glenn also said he had a nosebleed that would not stop after the injury, and the chart notes indicate that Glenn displayed some amnesia and would occasionally lose track of conversation. The physician also noted that Glenn had refused medication since his leave started. In the same chart notes the physician who examined Glenn after his leave recommended that Glenn have repeated convalescent furloughs after a three-week hospital stay where they would attempt to get Dilantin back in his system.

After that first leave, medical personnel noted that Glenn was drinking heavily and picking fights with other patients. Another EEG was ordered and performed on March 21st in which abnormal electrical activity was noted specifically in the right temporal region of Glenn's brain. This would explain Glenn's inability to follow conversation. Other behavioral side effects of temporal lobe injuries include impaired long-term memory, changes in affective behavior and changes in sexual behavior. Though the electrical signals in the right temporal region seemed to be of some concern to the neurologist, he interpreted the overall activity in Glenn's brain as essentially normal. Neurology decided that as an extra measure, they would perform a particularly painful archaic procedure called a pneumoencephalogram (PEG) to get a good view of the processes of Glenn's brain.

On April 2 nineteen fifty-one, Glenn was escorted to the neurosurgery wing of Letterman Hospital where spinal fluid was removed with a large hypodermic needle from the lumbar region of his spinal column. The space left by the extraction of fluid was immediately filled by an injection of oxygen allowing the structure of the brain to show up more clearly on an X-ray. Glenn's x-rays revealed no abnormalities.

According to research on the procedure, side effects rising from the PEG were severe. Someone who received this procedure would most certainly have massive long-term headaches coupled with sporadic vomiting. Because there was no synthetic replacement for spinal fluid, it took a good long time for the body to regenerate more. In fact, it could have taken two to three headache-riddled months before normal movement within the central nervous system was restored. In the end, the PEG was only useful in imaging the structures of the brain and could not pick up any images that would help tin assessing soft tissue damage.

On April 21, the EEG that had been previously ordered on April the second was finally performed on Glenn's brain. The neurologist who read the EEG described the electrical signals in Glenn's brain as mildly abnormal and referenced slow activity randomly occurring in the right posterior temporal area as well as irregular activity in the prefrontal cortex.

Nurses notes Between May of nineteen fifty-one and June of nineteen fifty-one state that Glenn took another leave on May 4, and came back on June 3, during which time he took no medication. Orders given after his return from leave stated that medical personnel needed to observe Glenn closely and give him Dilantin in correct doses. His medical chart during that time reflects the doses of Dilantin administered along with behavioural notes. A checkmark depicted the days that he took his Dilantin, and an "N" depicted the days he refused or was AWOL. According to chart notes, Glenn either refused his medication or was AWOL seventeen times in June.

There were two lab reports generated about Glenn in June. The first report talked about Glenn's blood alcohol level. According to the results, his body contained two and one half mg. alcohol per one ml. of blood. Another lab report generated on June 18th reported that a sample of Glenn's urine appeared cloudy with the presence of white blood cells. It is noted that Glenn went on leave again sometime in July and then again on August 27. After that, he received yet another EEG where the interpretation of the results indicated that the activity of Glenn's brainwaves were, "abnormal and suspicious of a right-sided abnormality." The findings stated that even though there was slow activity on the right side there seemed to be suppression of normal activity on the left as well.

Name _____ CARTER, Clara _____ Grade _____ Pvt _____ Ward K-2

Date _____ 2 April 1951 _____ 19 _____   Age 29

PREOPERATIVE DIAGNOSIS: Post-traumatic encephalopathy with headaches.

Postoperative Diagnosis: Same

OPERATION: Pneumoencephalogram

RECORD: The patient was given preoperative medication of demerol, atropine and nembutal and taken to the operating room where he was placed in a sitting position. He back was prepped with tincture of merthiolate. Two No. 18 needles were introduced into the L-4-5 and L-4-5 interspaces. A spinal-manometer was placed in one of the needles and the fluid pressure was approximately 210 mm. of water. This is approximately normal pressure with the fluid level coming to just above the cisterna magna. Approximately 110 cc. of clear cerebral spinal fluid was removed. There was no discoleration of the fluid. The fluid was replaced with oxygen and the needles removed. The patient was taken to the X-ray room where routine series of x-rays were made. No marked abnormalities of the ventricular system or the subarachnoid spaces was noted except that there might be some slight cortical atrophy. A further report will be made by the X-ray Department on the x-ray series. The patient withstood the procedure well and was taken to the ward without further difficulty.

Operation began _____ 1345 _____   Ended _____ 1400 _____

Operator _____ Capt Kendrick _____

Anesthetic _____

Anesthesia used _____ Demerol 75 mgm _____   Amount _____

Anesthetist _____ Capt Williams _____

Specimens forwarded to laboratory for examination:

JOHN J KENDRICK JR CAPTAIN   M. C.

Pneumoencephalogram

On September 28, nineteen fifty-one Captain Kendricks and two assistants from neurosurgery performed another craniotomy on Glenn. The surgery involved incising the tough leathery Dura Mater and then examining and stimulating Glenn's pre-frontal cortex. The second surgery was different from the one performed at the field hospital in that the first craniotomy performed on Glenn was while he was unconscious. The second surgery at Letterman required him to be awake for a good portion of the procedure. Throughout his life Glenn spoke about this experience and how helpless he felt being awake while, "They drilled through my skull and picked around through my brain." According to family members, Glenn later refused medical procedures that might have brought him some relief and perhaps prolonged his life because the second craniotomy terrified him so much.

The first thing the surgeons performing the second craniotomy did was to re-open the area of the bony defect and drill a bur hole just behind the bony defect so they could examine Glenn's frontal cortex. They then extended the bur hole so that it would become part of the bony defect. When Glenn's brain became visible, the surgical team noted that the Dura Mater was covered by a large fibrous scar. The surgeons opened the Dura in a horseshoe shape toward the midline of the brain on the right side. They wrote in surgical notes that, "The cerebral cortex was enlarged and plastered up against the Dura Mater." The surgical team then electrically stimulated some of the scar tissue they found atop the cortex to see if any rapid, irregular or unsynchronized contraction of muscle fibres occurred in specific areas of his body. If there were `rapid jerky fibrillations it would have indicated that the motor cortex was involved, however; they observed no fibrillations.

After the electric stimulation, Glenn was mercifully given

sodium pentothal so that he wouldn't have to consciously endure the rest of the procedure. While he was unconscious, surgeons proceeded to outline the scar tissue and remove as much as they could from both sides of his cerebral cortex.   The surgical notes indicate that the surgeons were hesitant to remove scar tissue that was close to the motor cortex and stated in the record that, "It's uncertain what would happen if the motor cortex was separated from the scar." They were also concerned that if they decided to remove the whole scar then they would have to remove more of the skull to get at the scar and make the bony defect larger.

After they removed the scar tissue and controlled the bleeding; the surgeons did two things that sealed Glenn's fate. First, they lined the area of the cerebral cortex they had been working on with Gelfoam® and then they sutured up the Dura Mater and replaced the bony defect in his skull with a tantalum plate so that his brain didn't have room to swell and heal.

Gel-foam was probably the worst thing they could have left on Glenn's brain. Gel-foam, was created by Upjohn laboratories and touted as a miracle absorption agent designed to stop bleeding on the battlefield. It was a relatively new discovery and had been around only since the end of World War II, which was about four years before Glenn left for Korea and too early to gather data of its impact on brains or other organs in closed areas. There would not be any real discussion of the effects of gel-foam and its roll in neurology for many years. The warnings are well stated now and can be viewed at;

http://media.pfizer.com/files/products/uspi_gelfoam_sponge..

"The packing or wadding of gel-foam, particularly within bony cavities is not recommended." This sort of use, Pfizer goes on to say, *"Should be avoided since the swelling of gel-foam to its original size may interfere with normal function and/or possibly result in*

compression necrosis (death) of surrounding tissues."

Following the obtaining of complete hemostasis, the area was then lined with gel-foam, the dura was sutured with interrupted sutures of 0000 silk; the bony defect was covered with a tantalum plate - the plate was put in place by four screws, and the scalp flap was then replaced, suturing the galea with interrupted sutures of 000 silk and the skin with interrupted sutures of 0000 silk. The patient withstood the procedure without difficulty and was returned to the ward in good condition.

Anesthesia was 1% procaine, local infiltration, until the electrical stimulation of the cortex was being carried out, and the patient was then put to sleep with I.V. sodium pentothal.

J. M. KENDRICK, Capt., MC,

Surgical report depicting the use of Gel Foam

PATHOLOGICAL REPORT

NAME OF LABORATORY	ACCESSION No.	DATE
Letterman Army Hospital	S-53056	4 October 1951

GROSS: Received in formalin are two irregular, ragged fragments of brain tissue, one measuring 1.5 x 1.7 x 3.2 cm. to which is attached a small silver clip. The smaller fragment measures 1 x 1.2 x 1.5 cm. The tissue sections with a firm, fleshy resistance revealing a stroma composed mostly of a yellowish-white, somewhat sclerotic tissue in which are occasional sulci lined with a narrow zone of translucent grey tissue which reachs a maximum of 2 mm. in thickness. Occasional areas of reddish-brown discoloration are seen which appear to be hemorrhage surrounding areas containing clips. Representative sections are embedded.

Pathology report on brain tissue after craniotomy

On October 2, Glenn was given another EEG. The

interpretation of that EEG described the activity in Glenn's brain as *definitely abnormal*. The previous EEG performed on August 27, described his brain activity as only slightly abnormal but the October EEG indicated that his brain functions had deteriorated significantly five days after the removal of a portion of the cortical scar and the packing of Gel Foam directly on top of his brain.

Glenn had yet Another EEG on October 26, and they again described the findings as *definitely abnormal*. The notes went on to say that the abnormal brain activity showed no evidence of improvement. In the mean time, Glenn's irritability was dramatically increasing after his second craniotomy and he suffered from intense headaches. Also on the increase were Glenn's aggression, alcohol consumption, brawling and seizures. There was no denying the marked changes in the intensity and frequency of Glenn's behaviours and symptoms after the second craniotomy.

The first physician to hint at the possibility that Glenn's brain could have sustained further damage from the second craniotomy was Lt. Col. Greenwood who originally wanted Glenn returned to duty shortly after his arrival at Letterman. Greenwood referred to the second surgery in a consultation record sent to the psychiatric clinic on Oct. 30th, in which he asked for an opinion about whether Glenn was responsible for his own behaviours such as excessive drinking and fighting. He asked for a psychiatric diagnosis and possible treatment for Glenn and suggested that he might have to be boarded (military jargon for institutionalized). Greenwood went on to state that "Patient had cortical removal of frontal scar and has had difficulty in stopping alcoholic beverages since." Soon after Greenwood's inquiry, they transferred Glenn to the psychiatric ward where he spent the majority of his time confined to the isolation or closed ward because of bad behaviour.

There is no record of how long Glenn stayed in the isolation ward, but a report generated On December 17, spoke of a psychiatric examination that he had under gone. During that examination, Major Green asked Glenn about his previous experiences and discovered Glenn had some difficulty with adjustments and a history of acting out and rebelling against authority as a teenager. Captain Green also said that Glenn's military record had been good and not like his civilian record at all. The final opinion from Captain Green was that Glenn showed no anxiety and no indication of neurotic or psychotic illness. He went on to say that, "Patient would not be benefited by psychiatric treatment and had no condition that would warrant his separation from the Army for psychiatric disease."

Glenn had yet another surgery on November 15. It was to address a massive infection in his scrotum. Even though Glenn's medical chart indicated ton June 17, nineteen fifty-one that there was clear evidence of an infection somewhere in his urinary tract system, there is no record of treatment for that infection in his medical charts. By the time he was prepped for surgery, Glenn's left testicle had swollen to nearly twice its normal size.

Glenn was sedated for the surgery and a physician by the name of Yount opened the area of his scrotum and removed infection from his left testicle. Chart notes state that the mass in his left scrotal vault was nodular with yellow cord-like tissue in which there was a lot of necrosis. It also states that the spermatic cord and vas deferens had some necrosis and scar tissue as well. Dr. Yount expressed his concern for the amount of necrosis and Glenn's future ability to produce and store sperm.

Progress notes from neurology dated December 10, indicated that Glenn remained neurologically asymptomatic and was given a thirty-day unsupervised leave and then was to return to duty afterwards.

According to chart notes dated January 14, nineteen fifty-two, Glenn had a seizure in the bathroom of the YMCA and was noisy, combative and incoherent afterwards. An ambulance picked Glenn up from the YMCA and took him to the emergency room at Letterman Hospital. In the chart notes from the Emergency Room, the doctor on duty stated restraints had to be placed on Glenn in order to prevent bodily harm to himself and to attendants. The doctor noted that he believed Glenn was hallucinating and reliving his war experiences. The ER doctor's name was Captain Peter Hogan and he could not get Glenn's charts right away, but managed to get a control card, which indicated Glenn had been shot and captured. From that little bit of information, Dr. Hogan surmised that Glenn was indeed re-enacting his capture by Chinese nationals. The doctor transferred Glenn to the S-1 (psychiatric closed ward) where even more effective restraints were applied.

For an hour and one half attendants and patients were held captive by Glenn's screams and vulgarities. The doctor seemed to have had a great deal of professional and personal concern about giving Glenn medication without viewing his chart first, but everyone has a breaking point and Dr. Hogan eventually embraced his and gave medication to Glenn. This could have come about by Dr. Hogan's great concern for Glenn's agitated state or much needed relief for the staff members and patients. Doctor Hogan noted that it was "not ideal" to give Glenn medication but after performing a precursory examination, the doctor concluded that he could not find any physical or neurological reason not to. Dr. Hogan administered five grams of Amytal, and Glenn immediately went to sleep.

The next day Glenn said he did not remember anything about the psychotic break and confessed to the doctor that he had been drinking and didn't take his medication. Glenn's chart did not arrive in the emergency ward until January 18. Captain Hogan reviewed the chart and decided that, since neurosurgical services made a determination that Glenn was fit for duty and had no psychiatric disease: Glenn should go to neurosurgical for final

Disposition

After the incident in the emergency room, Captain Walter Anglin (the same physician who gave Glenn leave and said he was fit for duty), wrote an opinion to Psychiatry. He essentially said that neurology had done all it could but the patient kept drinking and refused to take his Dilantin. He wrote that Glenn came back to neurology from Psychiatry and was then transferred to the closed ward. Dr. Anglin argued that Glenn's condition warranted psychiatric care. Captain Anglin also commented that He did not understand why psychiatric services would transfer Glenn back to neurological services and implied that maybe the good doctors in psychiatric services were just trying to pass Glenn off to his wing of the hospital because the patient was so difficult.

| Psychiatric Clinic | FROM: (Requesting ward, unit, or activity) Neurosurgery (Ext. 3140) | DATE OF REQUEST 30 October 1951 |

REASON FOR REQUEST (Complaints and findings)

Patient had cortical removal of right frontal scar. He has difficulty in stopping alcoholic beverages. Request opinion as to whether he is responsible.

More interested in psychiatric diagnosis & possible treatment. If needed, patient may have to be boarded.

DIVISIONAL DIAGNOSIS
GSW, penetrating, frontal skull.

Kendrick, Capt., MC — APPROVED — PLACE OF CONSULTATION: ☐ BEDSIDE ☒ ON CALL — ☒ ROUTINE ☐ EMERGENCY

CONSULTATION REPORT

Asking for psychiatric diagnosis

Captain Anglin's annoyance with Captain Hogan's transfer of Glenn to neurological services was evident in his correspondence. At the end of January, Captain Anglin wrote that Glenn's transfer to neurology was, "Never authorized." He also stated that he had taken steps to block efforts to return Glenn to neurology from ward 61. The captain went on to say that, "The chief of neurology feels that the patient should be returned to ward sixty-one for Proper disposition." It appears that Captain Anglin and Captain Hogan were playing a game of hot potato while Glenn remained in limbo and didn't recieve any services for his condition outside of medication and monitoring.

CLINICAL RECORD	CONSULTATION SHEET	
	REQUEST	
TO: SOCIAL WORK SERVICE	FROM: *(Requesting ward, unit, or activity)* Neurosurgery	DATE OF REQUEST 7 Feb 1952

REASON FOR REQUEST (Complaint and findings)

Patient had cortical removal of right frontal scar and suffers from post-traumatic convulsions. He has made poor adjustment during the latter part of his hospitalization and has been drinking to excess. This increases the severity of his convulsive seizures. Social Service requested to alleviate patient's drinking problem and promote better adjustment.

Glenn's referral to social services

In February of nineteen fifty-two, Lt. Javar from Neurosurgery services finally sent a request for consultation to Social Services. In his request, he made the same subtle correlation between the second craniotomy and Glenn's accelerated aggression and drinking by referring to his cortical scar removal and post-traumatic seizures. He went on to say, "Patient has made poor adjustment during the latter part of his hospitalization and has been drinking to excess." Lt. Javar requested that Social Services attempt to help alleviate Glenn's drinking problem and promote better adjustment.

From Feb. 14 through March and April of nineteen fifty-two, Glenn had regular clinical sessions with a medical social worker by the name of Evelyn Newman. Mrs. Newman wrote in consultation records that she first contacted Glenn in the prison ward on G-3. She stated that he was there because he had initiated a drunken fight with another patient. In her sessions with Glenn she discovered that he had some paranoia about fellow patients in the hospital and other soldiers whom he said, "You can't trust them." She also noted that despite these feelings he seemed to have been able to establish close relationships in the service especially with younger, more dependent soldiers.

Mrs. Newman went on to say that several times during their sessions Glenn complained that he felt he was losing his mind and was afraid of his own aggression and hostility. Her report states that Glenn admitted he had lost control of his behaviour and stated that he was easily irritated and unable to stop drinking and fighting. He also indicated that he had forgotten how to do many of the things that he used to be proficient at, like playing the guitar. Mrs. Newman noted that Glenn related easily to her as a mother figure and established a dependent relationship with her. She wrote that Glenn seemed to benefit from the sessions at first and stopped drinking for almost three weeks.

Mrs. Newman believed that Glenn's condition became worse during the prolonged stays in wards 61 and G-3 while Neurology and Psychiatric Services were arguing back and forth. She was clearly upset and states that, "During that period of time, patient received no medical treatment whatsoever while awaiting disposition." Mrs. Newman gave an assessment of her sessions with Glenn in which she wrote, "Patient has showed some insight and ability to use casework help but repeatedly shows limited ability to tolerate frustration."

In the chart notes generated during the period in which Glenn had stopped drinking and was taking his medication regularly, it states that Glenn talked about attempting suicide. One nurse's impression of Glenn documented in chart notes was that he was pleasant and cooperative which would have been noteworthy given his previous exploits in the hospital. The nurse quoted Glenn as saying, "I have a good many worries and problems." The nurse goes on to say, "Patient did not feel like discussing the matter and went to bed."   From May 3rd to May 11th nineteen fifty-two, chart notes indicated that Glenn remained quiet and cooperative. There was also a record of the disbursal of Glenn's medication, and in May, he did not refuse or miss his medication at any time.

On February 26th, Lt. Javer again sent a consultation sheet to Psychiatry. He asked them to write an opinion and forward suggestions. His reasons for the request were, "Patient seems to have severe personality disorder which may make him unsuitable for further military duty." He also wrote, "No further neurosurgical procedures are contemplated."

On May 14 of nineteen fifty-two, Captain Hood wrote that Glenn had been admitted to S-1 following an alcoholic brawl. He wrote, "Patient's mental situation was similar to that reported in previous records in that he was complaining considerably of nervous irritability and headaches." Captain Hood writes in his chart notes that Glenn was experiencing increased seizure activity, showed a complete lack of empathetic personification had accelerated his antisocial behaviour and displayed increased emotional instability. Captain Hood wrote that he believed Glenn would never be able to make an adequate adjustment back into the Army, and said Glenn's behaviours indicated Post-traumatic Personality Disorder which would warrant separation from the military.

On May 19, chart notes indicate that Glenn was transferred to the open ward again from the prison ward after the alcoholic brawl on March 14. There are not any chart notes generated in April of nineteen fifty-two.

In May, a clinical history was compiled as a precursory step to getting Glenn discharged from the military. Captain Hood of NP services presented Glenn's clinical history (In the Army, neurology and psychiatry worked so closely that they combined to become Neuropsychiatric or NP services). Glenn's report was organized into four sections which included Present Illness, Family history, Past and personal history and Course in the hospital. The fourth section, Course in the hospital, required two and one-quarter pages of the four-page report. At the end of the report, Captain Hood made a recommendation that, "Private Carter appear before the Physical Evaluation Board (PEB) for retirement from the service and be discharged to his own care.

The final determination as to whether a soldier was fit or unfit for duty exclusively focused upon his or her ability to perform the duty of a soldier, and the PEB made that final determination. The process to grant Glenn a medical discharge began with Captain Hood's clinical history and recommendation. The medical professionals then presented their case before a medical board. After the medical board reviewed the findings, they sent them to the PEB to make a final determination.

On May 28ᵗ nineteen fifty-two the acting chief of NP Services, Albert J. Glass, along with Captain Hood and Major Green presented Glenn's case before the medical disposition board. The first determination of the board was that Glenn was mentally competent. The medical board report then listed two approximate dates of origin for Glenn's physical incapacity. The first date referenced his original battlefield wound in November of nineteen fifty and the other referenced an event that occurred in October of nineteen fifty-one. Because the only activity that Glenn experienced in October of nineteen fifty-one(besides getting drunk and fighting) were two EEGs, and because the dates listed were approximate; the only conclusion that could be made was that it was referring to the second craniotomy on September 28, of nineteen fifty-one. The date on the operational report of the second craniotomy was also dated October 4, less than a week after surgery. The board listed the disability incurred in November of nineteen fifty as permanent, disabling, and contributory to the diagnosis of post-traumatic personality disorder. They listed the trauma from the October 4 surgery as permanent but not disabling and not contributory to Glenn's PTSD. The degree of severity attributed to the nineteen fifty event was recorded as moderate, and the nineteen fifty-one event was listed as degree not available (DNA). The report heavily infers that the second craniotomy had a significant debilitating effect on Glenn.

Glenn was officially separated from the Army on June 13, nineteen fifty-two. The reason for separation was stated as "permanent disability retirement." Glenn received a Combat Infantry Badge, a Purple Heart, a Korean Service Medal with two bronze campaign stars, a United Nations Service Ribbon and three hundred dollars and some change. From that point on, as far as the United States Army was concerned; Glenn would have to take charge of his own affairs even though key players must have known that it was going to be impossible for him to do that. I would also think that they must have known that setting him loose in the world without regular monitoring would have substantial consequences for not only him, but for the people he came in contact with as well. There weren't any other alternatives for the VA in nineteen fifty-two other than permanently boarding Glenn in a psychiatric facility which would have run afoul of Captain Hogan's assessment that he did not suffer from any psychiatric disease.

The PEB staff at Letterman Hospital were unquestionably professional and of good conscience. They proved that by identifying the second surgery as a contributing factor to Glenn's disability even though they didn't seem to know exactly why. NP services could have put all the blame on his war injury but didn't. It's obvious they were troubled watching Glenn deteriorate so rapidly after the second surgery.

CLINICAL RECORD	DOCTOR'S PROGRESS NOTES

13 Feb 62   Patient brought in litter to ER from _____ when
he suddenly became noisy, incoherent & uncooperative.
Patient was seen to become aware well of lecture, after
which he slid to the floor, frothed at the mouth, &
suddenly woke up & above behavior. When seen in
emergency room, patient had to be restrained to prevent
bodily harm to attendants & bystanders. He apparently
was suffering from the delusion that he had been
captured in battle from by Chinese Communists & acted
toward the personnel accordingly. His hospital record
could not be obtained as he had apparently been on
leave & chapel was in red medic action. However,
record card indicated a penetrating skull wound
in Dec. 1951, so that it is not improbable that
he was reliving an actual experience or at least
the emotions he would have liked to display
during a capture.

Emergency Room report

Standard Form 507
Promulgated August 1948
By Bureau of the Budget
Circular A—32

CLINICAL RECORD	Report on <u>SOCIAL SERVICE PROGRESS NOTES</u>
	or
	Continuation of S. F. ______
	(Strike out one line) (Specify type of examination or date)

(Sign and date)   MO: Lt. Javer
                   MSW: Evelyn Newman
                         12 Feb 1952

a very close friendship with another patient who was an extremely passive dependent, immature, 21 year old soldier. He felt safe with him and superior. He protected this patient and spoke of him as being as he was when he first came into service, ignorant of city ways and easily taken in. This relationship seems to have gratified his ego, as well as his feelings of being needed.

Several times during my sessions with him he complained that he felt that he was losing his mind, was afraid of his own aggression and hostility and sometimes when he went to a bar he felt everyone was looking at him. He feels himself to have changed a great deal because of his war experiences. He has lost control, is easily irritated and prone to fighting, and is unable to do many of the things that he used to be fairly proficient in, for example, guitar playing. Sometimes he feels as though he has lost his memory.

Evaluation of Treatment: Pvt. Carter related very easily and very soon established a dependent relationship to me. In part he was motivated by his us my interest to get him out of the Army. Initially he seemed to benefit from the sessions and for approximately 3 weeks stopped drinking. However, he was not able to maintain this for very long and he again began to show his difficulties with tolerating frustration by drinking and getting into fights. This basic problem, of course, was made more difficult for him during his prolonged period of hospitalization, particularly since his return from leave in November and during which period received no medical treatment while awaiting disposition.

During the beginning, focus was on patient's experiences in battle in order to permit him to re-assimilate his traumatic, combat experiences. He seemed to be able to use my support as that of a good, nonauthorative, accepting mother. During the latter part of this period focus has been on helping patient sift out for himself the realities in his environment which cause him to rebel against authority. Further attempt has been made to increase his self esteem and feelings of adequacy and to understand and gain better tolerance of his behavior. Patient has shown some insight and ability to use casework help, but repeatedly shows limited ability to tolerate frustration.

Evelyn Newman
Medical Social Worker

EN/ms D-16 May T-16 May 1952

Notes from Medical Social Worker Evelyn Newman

Psychiatric Ward Letterman Hospital

CHAPTER 8

Glenn age 24, the thousand mile stare

Home Again

_"Gage is fitful, irreverent, indulging at times in the grossest profanity…
capricious and vacillating"_

Dr. John Harlow describing his patient Phinneas Gage

A band was playing when Glenn and two other soldiers stepped off the plane at the small airport in Missoula Montana in May of nineteen fifty-two. Glenn's parents were there to welcome him along with veterans from the local VFW who shook hands and issued congratulatory salutations. It was the hero's welcome that Glenn deserved. According to sources, everyone was very happy to have Glenn back home and very proud of his service to his country.

Both Minnie and David had spoken previously to Glenn's doctors at Letterman about the possible changes in Glenn due to his injury, but it's not clear whether they fully realized what it would mean for them. Even though the medical staff at letterman couldn't predict future ramifications of Glenn's injury, I'm sure they tried to tell his family that Glenn was having substantial problems adjusting. The question is whether they told them he'd never get better.

Veterans who sustained traumatic brain injuries (TBIs) while serving in recent Middle East conflicts were not just given a check and told, "You're on your own buddy." Beginning in two thousand and seven, the VA implemented mandatory TBI screening for all Veterans that served in combat operations and were separated from active duty service after September 11, two thousand one. These soldiers are more closely monitored and receive more supervision than Glenn ever had. The Veterans Health Administration today has a Polytrauma System network (PSN) of care to treat Veterans with TBI. Currently there are 87 Polytrauma Support Clinic Teams (PSCT) located in VA hospitals across the country. The PSCTs provide specialized outpatient care. There is also a support network for family members dealing with the effects of TBI on their loved ones and on themselves. In nineteen fifty-two none of that existed. Glenn was only twenty years and three months when he sustained his initial injury and twenty-one years nine months when he was discharged from Letterman. According to the

National Academy of Sciences (NAC) the pre-frontal cortex of males typically don't mature until their mid twenties. Because Glenn was so young, his pre-frontal lobe maturation was more than likely not complete when he was injured, therefore; his psycho-social maturation would have been permanently suspended. This would explain why his family complained about him being "The Eternal Teenager."

After Glenn returned from Letterman, Harry's wife, Rita Carter, told me that he had difficulty accepting the changes he was seeing in his family and wanted everything to be the same as he remembered it. The biggest change for Glenn was that his brothers were not as accessible to him as they once had been. All three were married and had at least a couple of kids by the time Glenn returned from Letterman, but instead of accepting the fact that his brothers had evolved from muckrakers to family men he blamed his brother's wives for taking them away from him. After his return, Glenn apparently spent a great deal of time trying to drive a mammoth wedge between his brothers and their wives.

Rita Carter said that she had some real concerns about Glenn and the way he was trying to impact her marriage during that time. She said Glenn often pretended she didn't exist and was constantly egging Harry on to drink and carouse with him. When Glenn and Harry were younger they got into a lot of mischief and friends and family members said that they were the two Carter brothers most likely to end up incarcerated together. It seems Glenn couldn't understand why it should be any different after his return from Letterman just because Harry was married and had children.

In nineteen fifty-five, Harry accepted a job in Los Angeles, California. Rita Carter told me that it was the best decision they ever made as it took their family away from all the Carter Brothers, especially Glenn. After Harry left, Glenn turned his attentions to his other brothers. At the time Hugh was separated from his wife and living in Missoula and Gay bartended at a little bar on the edge of Missoula's Skid Row.

Glenn's family knew that many of Glenn's behaviours were service related, but listening to various accounts from family members; Glenn's immediate family would sometimes talk as though he would eventually get over it. They didn't know anything about how the pre-frontal cortex functioned, nor did they seem to fully understand that Glenn's brain was irreparably damaged and no amount of cajoling, shaming or butt-kicking was going to change that. The Carters, however, were practical hopeful people who anticipated Glenn's healing and tried to help him transition back into society. They definitely could not have imagined what was in store for them all.

Another of the most consistent complaints about Glenn after his return from Letterman was his excessively vulgar language. Of course, swearing wasn't uncommon for the Carter brothers, but every other word that came out of Glenn's mouth would make your ears ring and the church ladies blush. From what I've read, constant swearing is a by-product of damage to the language processing area in the left hemisphere of the brain which is probably why Glenn seemed unable to control it. At any rate, it was a great concern for Glenn's sister in-laws who were raising young impressionable children at the time.

In spite of the injuries to his brain, Glenn still seemed to have the ability to reason somewhat intelligently. Unfortunately, it promoted the misguided impression that he had control over what he did or said. Glenn would often get clobbered for saying something inappropriate and offensive to a stranger or act impulsively and put out a cigarette in someone's drink. He probably should have been wearing a sign on his back that said, "No impulse control," but back then nobody would have known what that meant.

It's speculative to say that the reason immature practical jokes became Glenn's stock and trade for the rest of his life was because of his brain injury and frontal lobes that hadn't all the way matured, but it is a reasonable theory given what's currently known about the functions of the pre-frontal cortex and the individual's transformation when they are damaged. Of course being the recipients of those immature pranks time after time exasperated his family. Because of Glenn's particular brand of brain damage, he also could not tolerate the slightest irritant and would strike out without hesitation. So whether angry, sad, excited or frustrated; all of Glenn's reactions to these emotions were out there for everyone to see in the most startling and sometimes vulgar and violent forms imaginable.

When I asked Mom about Glenn's impulsive behaviour she said that she had also observed Glenn overreacting to situations that someone with the ability to control their impulses probably wouldn't have reacted to at all. She described a time when she and Thelma and Glenn had decided to have a drink together and were sitting at the bar chatting when all of a sudden Glenn hauled off and hit the man sitting at the bar on the other side of him with a beer mug alongside his head just for moving his pack of cigarettes out of the way. Unfortunately, the man was much bigger than Glenn and started to come after him. Mom said that she and Thelma became alarmed and sprung into action. They started hitting and kicking the man from behind as he was swinging at Glenn. In the end, the police were called and Glenn, Mom and Thelma all went to jail. Nancy told me that Thelma's husband was not amused and did not understand why Thelma had to come to Glenn's rescue. A big battle between the couple took place with Gay intervening at some point.

Glenn also told his family that sometimes he would black out when he got angry and have no recollection of what he had just done. These blackouts came primarily when he was drinking heavily and occasionally when he wasn't, depending on the emotional reaction he was having. A blackout that came when he was experiencing an extreme emotional reaction was nearly always a precursor to some kind of violent physical altercation which would land Glenn in the lap of the authorities.

According to Nancy Carter, Glenn had been home from Letterman less than a month when he got into some trouble that involved the police. The police weren't called every time Glenn got into a fist fight but on this particular occasion, the barkeep reacted swiftly before his establishment was irreparably damaged. Within minutes after the fight started, two officers arrived and tried to take Glenn into custody. According to Gay's daughter, Nancy, Glenn started swinging and swearing and became particularly belligerent with one of the officers. Nancy states that one police officer in particular was not happy with the way Glenn was acting toward them so he put him in cuffs and took him down to the police station. When Glenn got to the police station, the police officer Glenn had gotten belligerent with at the bar tore into him and beat him severely with a Billy Club before word could get back to Gay, who would have come to Glenn's rescue earlier had he known his little brother was in trouble.

Nancy said that Gay was eventually able to make his way down to the police station to post bail for Glenn, but when he was escorted back to Glenn's cell; Gay found Glenn spread-eagle on the jail-house floor bleeding and battered. Gay, according to his daughter, was livid and tried to tell the arresting officer about Glenn's service to his country and about the injury to his head but the officer was impertinent and dismissive. I'm told that at one point Gay started to throw a few choice words the officer's way and the officer threatened to throw him into jail as well. Nancy said that Gay managed to calm down enough to avoid jail and get his brother home that night, but he would not forget the officer who gave his little brother such a severe beating.

Nancy said that Gay bided his time and asked around about the officer who had hurt Glenn and where he lived. She said that Gay also found out which taverns he routinely patronized then hid out along the officer's path and jumped him. Nancy said that Gay pounced on the officer and gave him a good beating and told him that if he touched his little brother again, all the Carter brothers would be paying him a visit. That officer never bothered Glenn again according to what Nancy Carter told me, and his family got the word out about Glenn and warned anyone who wanted to fight him that if they did so they would have to fight the brothers as well. Because of his brother's warnings, Glenn couldn't even pay someone to fight him and Mom said that infuriated him.

Proc Natl Acad Sci U S A. 2012 Oct 16; 109(Suppl 2): 17186–17193.
Published online 2012 Oct 8. doi: 10.1073/pnas.1121251109
https://www.polytrauma.va.gov/

Harry and Family leaving for California L-R Rita's uncle, Mom, Glenn, Harry with Jimmy in front of him, Rita, Thelma with Harry's oldest daughter and David Carter

CHAPTER 9

Mom, age 15

Edna May From Troy to Glenn

Whoever closes his ear to the cry of the poor will himself call out and not be answered."
Proverbs 21:13

James Applegate was not a good man. He brought my Grandmother and their four children to Troy, Montana in the spring of nineteen thirty-four then abandoned them that same winter. As if abandonment wasn't enough; my grandmother came to realize a month or so after Applegate's departure that she was pregnant again. Grandma wrote to her husband's family about her predicament, but there was never any reply. When the time came for Grandma to deliver my mother, a local midwife assisted. Grandma gave birth to Mom in August of nineteen thirty-five. She didn't apply for a birth certificate right away because there wasn't any father to sign it and it would have been marked illegitimate and brought a great deal of shame on both her and my Mother. Three years after Mom's birth, Grandma convinced a carpenter/handyman by the name of George Miller to marry her and then Grandma applied for Mom's birth certificate. George Miller signed the birth certificate and then gave Grandma all the money he had including the ten dollars it would cost to get a divorce and left town never to be seen again.

Shortly after George Miller left Troy, the state swooped in and took all four of Grandma's older children to the state orphanage/work farm in Twin Bridges Montana. It was not uncommon during the great depression for state agencies to take children away from their mothers if someone in the community issued a statement of concern, and that is what someone did to my Grandmother. My Mother did not meet the state's minimum age requirement to be at the work farm so she stayed with Grandma. Grandma would tell my mother later that having Mom with her was the only thing that kept her sane after the other four were taken.

Not long after the children left, Grandma and Mom were relocated by the city of Troy to a hastily constructed "Hooverville/ shanty village" down by the Kootenai River. They lived in that Hooverville for a little over a year until Grandma started cooking for timber camps in exchange for room and board.

STATE OF MONTANA
STANDARD CERTIFICATE OF BIRTH
State Board of Health
BUREAU OF VITAL STATISTICS

Original Record for State Registrar.

DO NOT WRITE IN THIS SPACE

Lin. 2778

Place of Birth
County of _Lincoln_
Village or City of _Troy, Mont._ No. _____ Street. Reg. No. _____
(If birth occurred in a hospital or institution, give its NAME instead of street and number)

2. Full name of child _Edna May Wadleigh Miller_

If birth is not yet named, make supplemental report, as directed

3. Sex _Female_
4. Twin, triplet, or other _____
5. Number, in order of birth _____
6. Premature _____
7. Legitimate? _X_
8. Date of birth _Aug 20 1900_ (Month, day, year)

FATHER

9. Full name _George Edward Miller_
10. Residence (usual place of abode) (If non-resident, give place and State) _Troy Mont_
11. Color or race _White_
12. Age at last birthday _49_ (Years)
13. Birthplace (city or place) _Waukesha Wis._ (State or country) _USA_
14. Trade, profession, or particular kind of work done, as Spinner, Sawyer, Bookkeeper, etc. _Forest Serv. Employ_
15. Industry or business in which work was done, as Silk Mill, Sawmill, Bank, etc. _Common Labor_
16. Date (month and year) last engaged in this work _Season of 1935_
17. Total time (years) spent in this work _one for 18th year_

MOTHER

18. Full name _Nina Wadleigh_
19. Residence (usual place of abode) (If non-resident, give place and State) _Troy Mont_
20. Color or race _White_
21. Age at last birthday _38_ (Years)
22. Birthplace (city or place) _Delmont_ (State or country) _So. Dak._
23. Trade, profession, or particular kind of work done, as Dressmaker, Typist, Nurse, Clerk, etc. _____
24. Industry or business in which work was done, as Own Home, Lawyer's Office, Silk Mill, etc. _____
25. Date (month and year) last engaged in this work _19_
26. Total time (years) spent in this work _____

27. Number of children of this mother _____

28. Stillborn, period of gestation _____
29. Cause of stillbirth _____

What prophylactic was used to prevent ophthalmia neonatorum? _____

CERTIFICATE OF ATTENDING PHYSICIAN OR MIDWIFE

I hereby certify that I attended the birth of this child, who was _Born alive_ at _____ m., on the date above stated
(Born alive or stillborn)

When there was no attending physician or midwife, then the father, householder, etc., should make this return.

Given name added from a supplemental report _____ (Date of)

(Signed) _(Supported by affidavit_ M.D.
or _of mother alone_ , Midwife
Address _____
Filed _2/7/39_, 19 _J M Clark_

Mom's birth certificate filed in 1939

For the little extras she and Mom needed, Grandma would take in laundry and sewing from the ladies that worked in the local brothels. This practice caused quite a stir with the locals I'm told and cemented a reputation Grandma certainly did not deserve.

Grandma was working and living in a lumber camp cook house up on the Yak River when she became better acquainted with Troy's only police officer, Jake Dietz. Grandma told Dietz about her children the state had taken from her and how desperate she was to have them returned to her. Because Dietz was interested in her, he told my grandmother that he'd help her get her children back if she'd agree to be his woman. Unfortunately for Grandma, Mom and the children at the work farm; Dietz lied.

Jake Dietz turned out to be a cruel drunkard and beat Grandma viciously, often in front of my mother. Once he had beaten her so severely that Grandma took Mom and Dietz's baby, Janice, and caught a ride with an acquaintance to Libby where she bought train tickets to California where her uncle lived. Unfortunately, Grandma only got as far as Walla Walla, Washington before collapsing and getting carried off the train by authorities and taken to St. Mary's hospital. Mom said she was nine years old when they took Grandma off that train. She also said that she and Janice stayed at the hospital while Grandma recovered and she earned her keep by scrubbing their floors. She did say that she thought the nuns were very nice to her because they gave her candy. When Grandma was well enough to go home, someone sent a telegraph to Jake Dietz after finding information about him among Grandma's personal items. He came and took them back to Troy.

Mom was forced to take Jake Dietz's last name but there was no mistaking the fact that she disliked the man intensely. Mom would never talk about all that he did to her, but a shadow would come across her face whenever she spoke of him. When the four oldest children were finally released from the work farm in the mid forties, Dietz was cruel to them as well and eventually ran them off the property. In the summer of nineteen fifty, mom whacked Dietz alongside of his head with the flat of a shovel as he walked through the back door of their house spitting and screaming about giving Grandma another beating. It was the last time Dietz ever set foot on their property. In September of that same year, Grandma and her children packed up all their earthly possessions and moved to Missoula.

Besides the insidious cruelty of Jake Dietz, my mother survived small pox, the great flood of nineteen forty-eight, starvation and pestilence; all of which made her determined to seek out a better life for herself as she got older. Once when she was six, she accidently got hit in the head and knocked out by a shovel someone was using to dig a slop hole. She said Grandma didn't stitch her up but doctored her with Lysol and used a butter knife to squeeze the wound together until it was healed. Mom also said she was dizzy and sick for several days after her accident.

Mom was raised in abject poverty, but Grandma had been raised in a well-regarded middle-class family. That made the kind of poverty my mother experienced situational and not generational. Nevertheless, Mom and her entire family were looked down upon by the better situated white town folk of Troy and Mom spent a good portion of her youthful energies trying to claw her way up from the bottom rung of the social ladder.

Mom said she also had to fend off aggression from kids who were better off than her. For the most part she could avoid them, but school was a different story. She said she endured a lot of hatefulness from kids who made fun of her because of the clothes she wore and the fact that she had to wear her brother's logging boots in the winter that were three sizes too big for her.

Mom said she developed a thick skin against the taunts of mean children, but couldn't abide anyone physically hurting her. She said there was a very mean boy in middle school who used to come up behind her and stab her in the shoulder with his pencil as hard as he could and run away chanting "Dietz Dietz with the big fat feets." Mom said it hurt like the dickens but it was also humiliating. In no time, Mom devised a plan to take care of that boy once and for all. She went home and sifted through the wood pile they kept in their back yard until she found a piece of lumber that satisfied her. She then borrowed some fabric from her mother's sewing basket and wrapped it around the block of wood to make it look as if it were a book with a homemade book cover on it.   The next day Mom walked down the hall clutching that disguised piece of wood and waited for that boy to come up behind her. When he did, she turned around and hit him alongside the head with that piece of wood as hard as she could. She said her tormentor fell to the floor and didn't move.

Like Thelma and Gay, Mom gained a great deal of respect for sticking up for herself, but unlike them; she nearly got thrown out of school. When she got called into the principal's office, she said he was as mad as a wet hen until she rolled up a sleeve and showed him one of her shoulders riddled with dozens of swollen grey pock marks.
She said the principal's eyes got as big as saucers when he saw all the holes in shoulder. He told her that he wasn't going to punish her but made her promise to talk to him first before she cold cocked someone. No matter how you look at it, my mother's childhood was very challenging. She worked hard for every penny and never backed down from a fight or missed an opportunity to make her situation better. Although Mom never said so directly, I always got the impression that she must have mistakenly thought that marrying Glenn would be a step up from her life in Troy.

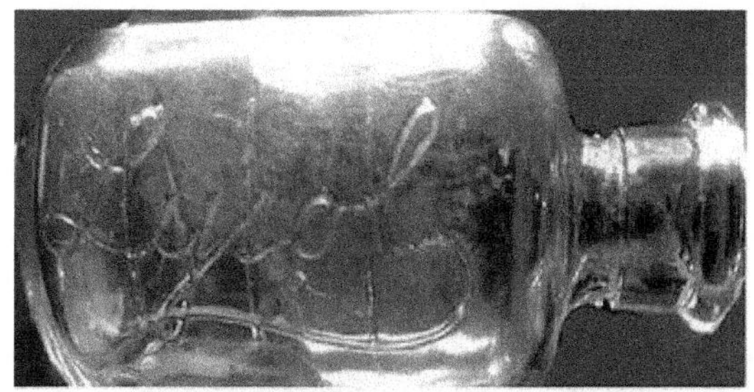

Lysol Bottle Mom found in Troy's city dump

Mom in her Flower Sack Dress
Down by the Kootenai 1938

Mom and Janice, Troy 1944

L-R Oren. Lowell, Lois and Neta Applegate at the
Children's Work Farm in
Twin Bridges Montana 1938

Glenn and Mom in 1953 before they were married

Glenn and Edna

The hardest part of dreaming about someone you love is having to wake up.
— Unknown

Mom was introduced to Glenn by her older brother, Oren. Oren had been hired to work at the Highlander Brewery in Missoula in October of nineteen fifty-one and then met Glenn Carter when he was hired on as a favour to his brother Gay in the summer of nineteen fifty-two. Mom said Oren used to tell them a lot of stories about Glenn before finally bringing him around to meet everyone. She said they were funny stories that often involved Glenn laying underneath an open tap and letting the contents of a beer keg pour into his mouth and out again until he was virtually lying in a pool of premium lager.

When Oren introduced Glenn to his seventeen year old sister, Edna May, she said she was swooning. Glenn was tall, extremely handsome and a veteran. It was the boyfriend trifecta a seventeen year old girl in the nineteen fifties would be looking for. It probably didn't matter to her that every other word coming out of Glenn's mouth was crude as she'd heard the same kind of language coming out of the mouths of the lumberjacks and Gandy dancers she'd been exposed to as a child living in Troy. The kind of brain damage Glenn lived with didn't make him appear too far out of the mainstream until you really got to know him. On the surface, Glenn didn't walk funny, or drool or give any outward indications that something was terribly wrong with him.

By the time my Mother became acquainted with Glenn, he had already acquired quite a reputation for chasing women, drinking, fighting and getting into trouble with the law; things my Mom was aware of but didn't know the breadth of initially. My mother's friend, Toke Jane, said that most of the decent and even some of the indecent young women in Missoula would cross the street just to avoid Glenn. She also said that she tried her best to warn my Mother about him but it didn't matter because Mom was convinced Glenn wasn't as bad as people thought.

Members of Glenn's family told me that Glenn having a steady girl lik Mom was a relief for his parents and siblings who were trying desperately to help him assimilate back into polite society. Having a girlfriend also helped take some of Glenn's focus away from his brothers. Glenn's family was very happy to welcome Mom into the fold, and it didn't take long for my mother to fall in love with his family as well. Mom always spoke about Glenn's family with great affection, especially for his parents and for the Carter women. She told me that Thelma and the other sister-in laws were very kind to her and were, "So beautiful they could have been in movies."

Mom never really wanted to talk about her and Glenn's courtship. I think she might have been embarrassed to speak about how badly she let him treat her. I did find a note in one of her scrapbooks from Glenn apologizing for tearing up one of her photo albums during that time. It also included my mother's response stating that she probably deserved it and she could never stay mad at him. Though the details of their courtship have always been a mystery, it's a fact that while they were running together; my mother and father's relationship became physical. It seems that losing the function of one of his testes while at Letterman Hospital did little to deter Glenn's virility because he managed to impregnate my mother in June of nineteen fifty-three.

Mom always tried to keep the truth about being pregnant before her marriage from my sister and I. She was so ashamed of that fact that she went to extraordinary lengths to conceal it from us by altering my sister's birth certificate. In those days they put the marriage date of the couple on their child's birth certificate and Mom had scratched out the original date and put in, "nineteen fifty-two" below it. When the truth came out, Mom exploded in a tirade and announced that Glenn had, in fact, raped her.

Whether Glenn violated Mom or she just fabricated the story out of desperation to ease her shame and guilt about it; I'll never know. What I do know is that my grandmother was furious when she found out about my Mom's pregnancy, and put much of the blame on my mother. Nancy Carter told me that my Grandma actually paid a visit to the Carter household after finding out about Mom's pregnancy and cursed at them while offering up colourful opinions of their youngest son's behaviour. Grandma did not hold back when she was upset. I can still remember how her sharp salty tongue would slice and dice with precision when expressing a deep displeasure.

Mom and Glenn were married on Halloween night, nineteen fifty-three in Hamilton Montana. Four months later, Myra Kay was born at St. Patrick's Hospital in Missoula.

According to my mother, Glenn was pleased with little Myra Kay but was still compelled to act on his impulses which often persuaded him to chase other women, drink excessively and get into fights.

Six weeks after Myra was born, my mother went back to work cooking at the Minute Kitchen restaurant where she had been employed before giving birth. Even though Glenn was receiving a sizeable VA check each month, Mom said he did not let her have any of it. Instead, he spent almost all of it on alcohol and luxury items like leather jackets. Rita Carter told me that because leather jackets were very popular in the fifties Glenn felt he had to have one. She said it was both comical and sad how nearly every month he would routinely buy an expensive new leather jacket and then end up pawning it toward the end of the month for more drinking money.

Mom's job at The Minute Kitchen paid the rent and utilities, but she said there wasn't much left for anything else. The Minute Kitchen was owned by a man named Bill Hayline, a very prominent businessperson in Missoula at the time. Mom always described Mr. Hayline as a good and fair employer who sometimes let her take left-over food home. Mom said that for milk and cigarette money, she would take the change out of Glenn's pockets on the rare occasions he did come home to pass out after a night of drinking. She said Glenn never missed the money because she never took all of it and he couldn't ever remember what he'd done the night before. If my Mother was anything, she was resourceful and knew how to get what she needed. It seems to me that all the lessons life spit at my mother when she was young gave her the tools to survive Glenn. I'm sure her marriage to Glenn must have seemed just like another chapter of craziness in a lifetime of nothing but the same.

Glenn, Mom and little Myra Kay 1954

CHAPTER 11

New Arrival

Do ye hear the children weeping, O my brothers,
Ere the sorrow comes with years ?
They are leaning their young heads against their mothers, —
And that cannot stop their tears.

The Cry of the Children by Elizabeth Barrett Browning

In the winter of nineteen fifty-four, Mom was pregnant again and this time Glenn was far from pleased. Mom said he would brood and pontificate about it constantly. My mother states that she ignored Glenn's accusations and rants for the most part, but also stated that he did get a hold of her once and slapped her around pretty good while she was pregnant.

This altercation happened after Mom and Glenn had moved out of David and Minnie's house, and were living in an upstairs apartment on Cooper Street in Missoula. Mom told me that Glenn had come home perfectly sober one day and started screaming at her about infidelity while slapping her face and the sides of her head. Mom said the landlady downstairs heard the goings on and called the police.

When the police arrived, they took Glenn aside and had a talk with him because that is how they handled domestic violence calls in nineteen fifty-five. Mom said she knew Glenn would just go back to slapping her around after the police left, so while the police had Glenn occupied; Mom hurried downstairs and used the landlady's phone to call Hugh Carter and ask him to come get Glenn.

Mom said Hugh got to the apartment just as the police were leaving and tore into Glenn. He slapped Glenn just like Glenn had done to Mom then yelled at him and pushed him down a few times before forcing him into his car and taking him over to David's house. Glenn's normally calm and peaceful brother must have made an impression on him because Mom said Glenn didn't lay a finger on her throughout the rest of her pregnancy.

Physical violence wasn't unheard of in the culture both Mom and Glenn were a part of, and it most certainly wasn't something either of them shied away from if they felt the situation called for it. There's a story Mom's friend, Toke Jane, loved to tell about my mother and father's relationship that I've heard several times over the years. She begins the story by describing how she was walking home from work one night and came upon a crowd gathered together around a fight of some sort, but the circle around the fight was so tight that she couldn't see who was battling. All of a sudden, she said my mother's fringed leather buckskin jacket flew out of the fracas and she became very concerned and asked people around the outer rim of the circle just who was fighting. Toke Jane said that her worst fear was confirmed when the answer came back, "Glenn and Edna." She then said she started crying, "Someone stop it!" The man in front of her then turned around, looked at her hard and asked; "Why should we stop it when Edna's winning?"

Mom said she never started a fight in her life but she had to fight sometimes because that was the way things worked back then. She told us how she got pretty good at picking up a bar stool with one hand and hitting a masher over the head with it when she needed to. I remember entering my parent's bedroom one morning when I was around fourteen to borrow a pair of earrings from Mom's jewellery box and was startled to see Mom's upper denture plate sitting on top of it with two teeth missing. Mom only took her dentures out at night to place them in a glass filled with water and Efferdent, so seeing one on top of her jewellery box was not only startling; I found the thought of touching them repulsive and decided I didn't need to wear earrings that day. When I inquired about the toothless denture Mom told me that she and Dad got into an argument with another couple while playing shuffle board at a local bar in Kalispell the night before. She said it was just a war of words until the woman sucker punched her and knocked a couple teeth out of her upper denture plate. Of course I was snickering the whole time she was explaining this to me because it seemed so comical to see my mother with her cheeks drawn in trying to explain in her toothless dialect what had happened the night before. Mom gave me a look that seemed to say, "Get over yourself," and finished her explanation by declaring that the woman who hurt her probably wished she'd never done that.

I will never completely know how much abuse Glenn heaped on my Mother or me as I have few poignant memories of him outside of the frequent night terrors I experienced as a small child. There is one memory I have, however, that has been with me all my life. I remember my father wearing a white T-shirt and taunting me while opening and closing the door of a refrigerator that I was sitting in. I must have been around three years old but I can still remember seeing him smile at me each time he opened and closed the refrigerator door and feeling the cold rungs of the refrigerator shelf through my underwear as I sat there nearly naked and too terrified to move.

Another early memory I have is of Glenn walking briskly out the back door of our house in his birthday suit. My sister and I were sitting on the grass by the fence that separated our property from the neighbours just watching him as he marched out the back door.pointed his finger at Mom and started yelling. I remember that my Mother was in a skirt and blouse with her back to him and appeared to be trying to ignore him. I can also remember another instance where I scurried away from loud angry voices and hid underneath an ironing board much like a small animal would run for cover when frightened.

I know the police sometimes had to come and get Glenn out of the house when he got out of control. By association, my young mind conjured up an unhealthy fear of uniformed officers that stayed with me well into early adulthood. I can remember a time when I was five years old sitting in a booth at a restaurant across from my mother and future stepfather and a police officer walked in through the glass door at the front of the restaurant. I didn't know why, but an instinctual fear took hold of me and I slid under the table of our booth. My mother was very embarrassed and tried to pull me out from under the table, but even the threat of a spanking couldn't get me out from under that table until after the officer had left. My mother held on and endured Glenn's antics until the day he slammed the side of my face into the kitchen counter and fractured the orbit of my eye. I was three and one half years old.

Mom might have left Glenn long before he hurt me so badly, but the lure of his doting family, societal pressure and her belief that she could somehow handle him kept her in that situation much longer than she should have been. Glenn and Mom were married just over five years. After my mother left Glenn, she told me that the landlady downstairs expressed how relieved she was that Glenn wasn't on the premises anymore because she didn't know if she could stand listening to the baby screaming anymore when Mom wasn't there.   I had nightmares about my father at a very young age and I didn't understand how to sort it all out at the time, but the images from those dreams have always stayed with me. I realize now that the disturbing images from my dreams would have been impossible for a child to interpret but would be easily deciphered by an adult.

Myra Kay and Merrie Kathleen 1958

CHAPTER 12

AMERICAN LAKE

"Crows would get so drunk on fermented mulberries that they could get only one wing to flap at a time, and when it did get airbome it flew to the top of a building, crashed into the roof and then slid down and got caught on a gutter." Patients at American Lake hospital got a huge kick out of watching the crows."

David Nellis, American Lake's former gardener of 37 years,

Minnie Pearl Carter succumbed to cancer in nineteen fifty-eight. Rita Carter told me that Minnie was at the old post-office in downtown Missoula when she tripped going up some stairs and broke her left leg. She said Minnie was taken to community hospital where an X-ray of her leg revealed a tumour attached to one of her lower leg bones. The doctor who treated her wrapped her leg in a cast and sent her home. Minnie returned to the hospital a few days later and additional x-rays were taken of various parts of her body. The x-rays revealed at least three more tumors or osteosarcomas in her pelvis and right leg. Soon after that they put Minnie in a full body cast and sent her home. She remained in that cast until her death on January 7, nineteen fifty-eight.

Minnie's death devastated her family, but none more than Glenn who had remained especially close to his mother and whose death took away an essential part of his support network. Like any good mother, Minnie embraced Glenn unconditionally and tried to assist and protect him after his release from Letterman. Glenn found refuge in Minnie when everything else was crumbling around him and his siblings were not available to him. She helped ease the loneliness and isolation he was feeling as a result of his irrational and often violent behaviour. When Glenn first returned home from Letterman she was hopeful that he would eventually revert back to his old self, but when it became obvious that it wasn't going to happen; Minnie grieved deeply. Hugh Carter wrote in one of his letters to Mom that, "Glenn not only lost a mother, he lost his best friend."

About six months after Minnie's death, David Carter moved to Brush Prairie, Washington. Glenn followed David there after it became apparent Mom wanted nothing more to do with him. David and Minnie had friends and relatives in Brush Prairie but Hugh's wife, Janet, once told me that part of David's reason for wanting to move away from Missoula in the first place was Glenn. Janet said that Minnie had always dealt with Glenn after his return from Letterman and David didn't get involved with his antics as much and really didn't care to. Glenn, of course, couldn't understand how he was impacting his father with his behaviour. Not long after Glenn arrived in Brush Prairie, David packed up and moved back to Missoula.

While in Brush Prairie, Glenn started dating a woman of Hispanic origin. He had been seeing her for a few months and had started living with her after his dad left. Glenn also kept up correspondence with my mother during that time and for some unexplained reason started to nurture the hope that she would come back to him. Of course, the relationship between Glenn and the Hispanic woman began to deteriorate once she found out that Glenn was trying to reunite with my mother. It then ended abruptly and violently according to a letter that Hugh Carter wrote to my Mother. Hugh and his wife, Janet, had reconciled by then and lived in Vancouver, Washington when he sent that letter to my mother in nineteen fifty-nine. Hugh stated that Glenn was excited about the notion that my mother was coming to visit him and perhaps stay and said that he went over to the apartment he was sharing with the young Hispanic woman to retrieve some of his belongings. Glenn told Hugh he was packing up and the young Hispanic woman got upset and started screaming at him and saying some unsavoury things about my mother which triggered a very dangerous response from Glenn.

Glenn told Hugh that he became so mad that he blacked out and couldn't remember nearly beating the poor woman to death afterwards. When Glenn regained his senses and saw what he had done to the woman, he contacted Hugh who convinced him to turn himself into the authorities. The young Hispanic woman was taken to the hospital by ambulance and filed a complaint against Glenn there.

As soon as Glenn turned himself in, he was booked and put in a jail cell. Shortly after, a sheriff's deputy found him hanging in his cell with bed sheets tied around his neck. The deputy immediately performed artificial respiration on Glenn and when he regained consciousness he told his jailers, "Do something with me before I kill someone." In his previous clinical notes, Glenn stated that he was afraid of the rage inside himself, so making a plea for someone to do something with him before he killed someone was just another confirmation of that fear.

In lieu of sending Glenn to prison, Hugh signed papers to have him committed to the VA mental hospital at American Lake for an indefinite period of time. In a letter to my mother, Hugh spoke of tremendous guilt on the part of himself and his siblings for not paying enough attention to Glenn. Hugh and Thelma also pleaded with my mother to write to Glenn and consider visiting him while he was in the hospital. Gay's wife, Dusty, wrote to my mother during that time and told her how relieved she was that Mom had decided not to reunite with Glenn.

Suicide Attempted

VANCOUVER — A suicide attempt by a prisoner at the Clark county jail was thwarted Wednesday night by a jailer, Sheriff Clarence S. McKay reported Thursday morning.

The jailer, Albert Forgey, used artificial respiration to revive Glenn A. Carter, 28, Brush Prairie, after he found the man hanging in his cell. The man had used bedding as a rope in the unsuccessful attempt, the sheriff said.

Carter was later taken to the county hospital after being checked by a doctor.

He had been placed in the jail's hospital cell following his arrest earlier in the evening on a warrant charging him with assaulting a Brush Prairie woman.

Newspaper article about Glenn's suicide attempt

After Glenn's suicide attempt, Hugh and Thelma wrote to my mother. His brother Hugh wrote, "There were many of Glenn's friends at his trial and I didn't realize he had so many friends." It was also noted in Glenn's VA records that he had a few friends in spite of his fights and antisocial behaviour. Most of Glenn's friends were men, like him, who had served their country in the armed forces and were never the same for their experiences. She told Mom that Glenn had experienced a break down and said he had been taken to an Army Mental hospital and nobody was allowed to visit or talk to him for awhile. She also encouraged Mom not to blame herself because Glenn's break down had been coming long before she met him.

After Hugh's first letter was sent, a team of psychiatric professionals and social workers from American Lake hospital sat down with Hugh and Thelma to impress upon them in terms they could understand, just how impacted Glenn was by his brain injury and how dangerous he was. After that sit-down, Hugh wrote to my Mother telling her that he understood why she would not want anything to do with Glenn and that she should not feel bad about it. He also reiterated that he and his siblings had not understood Glenn nor helped him near enough.

If I know one thing about Glenn's brothers and sister, it is that they loved their little brother deeply. This is evident in every single document I've read and throughout all the personal testimony I've gleaned from surviving family members. They had difficulty, however, inviting the kind of behaviour they were seeing in him (even knowing it wasn't his fault) into their homes and around their children. They had valid concerns about their children's exposure to Glenn's constant oral vulgarities, impulsive unpredictable emotions, violent temper and inappropriate practical jokes. When he was drinking, those bizarre unpredictable behaviours were amplified tenfold. In addition, because nobody could force Glenn to take his seizure medication regularly; it created additional anxiety for family members who feared that he might scare or unintentionally hurt one of their children during a seizure. Glenn spent approximately seven months at American Lake and then returned to Missoula to live with his father again. Glenn's first thought upon arriving in Missoula was to visit Mom, and I remember that visit well.

Mom, Grandma, Janice and I had just been released from the month long quarantine imposed on us after Myra was diagnosed with Polio. My grandmother, a devout Jehovah Witness, did not want Mom to take Myra to the hospital in the first place and did everything she could to dissuade her from doing that. Grandma was certain that all Myra needed was some of her herbal poultices and worried that once in the hospital Myra might never come home again. She would talk about what she perceived as Mom's folly over and over again during their period of confinement and cursed Toke Jane for taking Mom and Myra to the hospital even though it took a lot of courage for Toke Jane to do that and expose her two young sons to whatever it was that Myra had.

Those days of quarantine had been very hard for all of us but I think for me especially. I was still trying to recover from the trauma I experienced being in the same household as Glenn when Myra became ill. The quarantine imposed by the health department just made all the adults around me short tempered and made me even more afraid and withdrawn. I realize now that the tension and grief they were feeling must have been intolerable and they can't be held responsible for any impatience they showed for me during that time.

Eight days before the quarantine was lifted, Myra was taken out of the iron lung. Two days after the quarantine was lifted my grandmother took me with her to get her hair fixed by someone she knew that lived in town. It was during that walk to town that a very curious thing happened to me. I remember the day was dreary, dirty snow was hugging the curbs and Grandma had a tight grip on my hand and was pulling me along. She only made on stop, and that was in front of St. Francis Xavier Catholic church to adjust her stockings. Of course she had to let go of my hand in order to make her wardrobe adjustment and as she did, I turned my attention to the big wrought iron fence that surrounded the church-yard and went over and pressed my face between the bars to get a look. What I saw was a life-size replica of David's Pieta sitting in a sleeping garden off to my left, and what I felt while looking in at the statue can only be described a supernatural.

As I stared in the direction of the lovely stature, I felt a sensation like someone completely wrapping me up in a blanket of indescribably joy and peace. I don't know why, but I knew that it wasn't just a feeling, it was a form of communication and there was someone in the churchyard doing that to me. I remember wanting so badly to squeeze those wrought iron bars to find that person. It was uncharacteristic of the very frightened and withdrawn little girl I had become. I didn't know then what to make of it all, but after Grandma told me that the lovely statue in the churchyard was of a man named Jesus, I was pretty sure that he was the one hugging me that day.

I didn't recognize Glenn when he came to our house that day but didn't run away from him and hide under my bed like my mother said I had less than a year earlier. I remember walking into the kitchen and seeing Glenn sitting on a chair next to the back door with his right arm resting on the kitchen table. Even though I didn't know who he was, he was near my Mother and seemed friendly enough. Glenn smiled and beckoned for me to come to him but I didn't move until my Mother, who had her back to me, turned her head to look at me and tell me that it was all right. I went to Glenn, climbed on his lap and immediately noticed his thumb was missing its top half. I had recently had a run-in with a trashcan lid that fell on my big toe and cut it severely so I asked him if his thumb had encountered a similar fate. He talked loudly and smiled broadly saying, "That's what happened all right." Years later Mom told me he had cut that part of his thumb off working at a saw mill.

I recall my mother quietly watching Glenn as he interacted with me and bounced me playfully on his knee. In retrospect, it seemed like a big show that Glenn was performing for my Mother who was quietly watching from the wings. I might have asked him if he would like to push me on the swing in our backyard because we all moved outside and Glenn did start pushing me back and forth on the little swing that was part of our swing-set. I kept saying, "Push me push me," and he did. My mother watched briefly and then turned around and walked back into the house. As soon as Mom started walking back into the house, Glenn stopped pushing me and when I repeated "push me" he turned around and looked at me hard and said, "No." The tone of his voice terrified me and I put my head down so I didn't have to look at him. I sat quietly frozen to my swing until he walked away. Something deep inside me recognized that tone of voice and I knew it wasn't safe for me. I stayed in the backyard until I could see my mother and Glenn get up from the table and walk into the living room. When I spied my grandmother walk into the kitchen; only then did I feel it was safe enough to go back into the house.

My mother told me some years later that my Grandmother had returned from an errand at that particular time and wasn't very happy to see Glenn. Mom said she took the hint and they went outside for a walk around the block together. It was during their walk around the block that my mother says Glenn expressed his extreme displeasure with her for not writing him or visiting him while he was at American Lake. He didn't accept the fact that Mom was hampered from doing so because Myra was in an iron lung and we were in quarantine, and told her that he had a mind to kill her. My Mother said he then came up behind her with his hands cupped ready to grab her neck and that's when she turned around, looked at him intently and said, "Go ahead and put me out of my misery."

My poor mother was in such a difficult situation during that time what with Myra in the hospital and having to work forty hours over the hot steam presses at Missoula Laundry to support us all, that I suppose she thought a crazy dangerous ex-husband might be the least of her worries. My mother said that after facing him down, Glenn seemed to sense the sincerity of her misery and changed direction. She said he walked along behind her silently for a while and then told her that he was going to California to visit his brother, Harry, who said he had a job for him. Then he warned Mom that if she should get any notions about other men or getting married again he'd find her and he'd kill her.

Myra home from St. Patricks Hospital 1960

July 27, 1959

Hi Edna,

Just a few lines to let you know what is happening out here as far as Glenn is concerned. I don't know how much he has told you about his private affairs but I do feel that I probably had better explain the difficulty he is in at the present time.

As he undoubtedly told you prior to his getting in touch with you again he was going around with this gal that lives out where he and dad were living in Brush Prairie. When he felt that you and the kids were coming out to see him he went over to her house to get back a few things that he had loaned her. She got mad and made some sassy crack about you and Glenn tells me he blacked out and proceeded to work her over. He went over and call the sheriff to come and get him and the gal also made a mad dash for a judge and swore out a warrant for him. The took him to the county jail and locked him up. They left him for a few minutes and when they came back he was hang -ing by his neck with the bedsheets. They cut him down an applied artificial respiration and brought him around but he kept telling them to do something with him Before he killed someone. All this happened Wednesday night and I was just allowed to see him yesterday which was Sunday.

I had to sign papers for a mental hearing which will be held the 29th which is the day after tomorrow. It is about the only out I had in order to keep him out of jail and I feel that is really for the best. If the doctors al agree they will try to get him to the V.A. Hospital at American Lake up by Tacoma. I have called sis and she wil be there. Glenn has changed quite a bit since you and he split up as you surely have seen. He has been doing real good in school and was going real steady over there. The only time he missed was when he took a few days off on the 4th of July to come over and see you and the kids.

I don't know what you kids had in mind in way of getting together again but If you were actually planning on trying it again for god's sake don't desert Glenn now because if he ever needed someone to lean on he really needs someone now. I hope it doesn't upset you too much

First half of Hugh's Letter

but the poor kid is on his last leg right now. He said
that the reason he tried to hang himself was because he
thought he might have killed that gal and he really
could'nt remember what he did after he blacked out.

I know he has done a lot of drinking in the past
and a lot of other things I hav'nt approved of but I
feel that he surely hasn't been understood by any of
his family and that includes me. I had a good long chat
with his doctor and beleive me I sure didn't think too
much of myself afterwards. I know I should have over
looked a lot of Glenns faults and tried to praise him
about a few of the good things he has done but I guess
I am just like the rest of the family and was too busy
trying to take care of my own kids etc and just didn't
have any time to devote to Glenn. I know he must have
been lonesome as hell out here after dad left and I
should have tried to see him more but I did'nt and just
look what happened. If you should blame anyone for the
pickle he is in Edna, just blame me and the rest of his
brothers and sister. I don't know your address so I am
writing this in care of dad and hope he will get in con-
-tact with you. Please will you write to Glenn in care
of me and I will see that he gets all your letters. I
would appreciate hearing from you and knowing your in-
-tentions so I will know how to talk to Glenn.

As always

Hugh

Hugh Carter
9700 N.W. 27th. Ave.
Vancouver, Washington

I don't know what you kids had in mind in way of
getting together again but if you were actually planning
on trying it again for god's sake don't desert Glenn now
because if he ever needed someone to lean on he really
needs someone now. I hope it does'nt upset you too much

Second half of Letter from Hugh.

Left to right

Skinny,Thelma,Karen,Karen's husband,Grandpa Carter,
Glenn and Gene.

<u>Gene</u>

It is pleasant, indeed, while the summer lasts
with the mild pheasants' song ...
but now I feel the northern wind's blast—
its severe weather strong.
Alas! Alas! This night seems so long!
And I, because of my momentous wrong
now grieve, mourn and fast.

Old English Lyric 13 AD

Glenn left Missoula a few days after his volatile visit with my mother and journeyed down to visit his brother, Harry, in Los Angeles just like he told Mom he was going to. Harry was not in attendance when social workers briefed Hugh and Thelma on Glenn's condition so he didn't get the full impact of what they were saying about him. Harry did have a second hand conversation with his sister, but I have to wonder if that would have impacted him as much as hearing it directly from medical personnel because he went ahead and invited Glenn to come down to California to stay with him and his young family as long as he needed to. Unfortunately, Harry failed to consult with his wife, Rita, before extending that invitation.

Rita Carter's exact words to me were, "I nearly had a heart attack when that taxi pulled up in front of my house and Glenn stepped out with all his worldly possessions." Rita knew that Harry, Hugh, Gay and Thelma were desperate for ways to help Glenn after he left American Lake but she sure did not expect that Harry would invite him down without telling her first.

Besides two suitcases stuffed with clothes, Rita said Glenn also had two bags of pills. Rita was an RN and was naturally curious about those pills, so she investigated them and said that one bag was full of Dexedrine and one was full of Milltown. Dexedrine was and is still a popular stimulant used to increase focus and ameliorate the affects of ADHD. Milltown was a widely used sedative which was later replaced by a class of drugs called benzodiazepines. The fact that Glenn had these bootlegged drugs seems to indicate that he was trying to self medicate in order to ameliorate some of the bizarre behaviors caused by the damage to his pre-frontal cortex; the behaviors that were getting him into trouble and making him suicidal.

Rita said she tried to lay down the law right away with Glenn about what he could and couldn't do in their house around their kids, but Glenn wasn't about to start paying attention to what a brother stealing wife had to say. She said it was Harry who had to speak to him about the concerns she had. Rita said there was little she could do after Glenn got there but devise ways to protect her young impressionable children from his erratic behaviors.

According to Rita, there were two things that Glenn did that she found unacceptable for her children. She said that Glenn would try to buy the affections of her children by taking them to the candy store nearly every day. She tried to tell him it was bad for their teeth and affected their appetites, but he wouldn't listen until Harry had a talk with him. Rita was also very concerned about Glenn's excessively colorful language around her children but knew it was completely out of his control. Aside from trying his hardest to give her children cavities and a more robust vocabulary; the fact that he had just been released from American Lake VA hospital after nearly beating a woman to death also weighed heavy on Rita's mind.

Besides the immediate concerns that Rita had, there was also one big concern that set off alarm bells for Thelma and Skinny. Their son, Gene, lived in North Hollywood at the time with his young wife and baby not far from Harry and his family. According to Rita, Gene's folks were not happy about Glenn being so close in proximity to Gene because they knew Gene had always looked up to Glenn and Glenn still had the ability to wield some influence over him. Thelma was particularly concerned after having that sit down with Glenn's doctors at American lake and coming to the realization that Glenn really did not have a lot of control over his destructive impulses. Thelma knew her son could be influenced by his uncle Glenn so she called and spoke to Glenn and warned him to stay away from Gene and his family.

Harry was the one who laid down the law and told Glenn that they would kick him out of their house if he tried to visit

Gene alone while he was living there. Both Rita and Harry made it a point to monitor Glenn's comings and goings as much as they could after that and made him report to them when he got a notion to go somewhere.

After about two weeks at Harry and Rita's house Glenn still hadn't secured a job and was getting restless, so he told Rita and Harry that he was going to take a bus and see his old service buddy, Bill, in Long Beach. Bill Johnson hailed from Missoula and had been one of the local vets who greeted Glenn when he first got off of the plane from Letterman. Bill was also a wounded veteran paralyzed from the waist down, and he and Glenn had become good friends. Mom once told me that Bill Johnson looked after Glenn those first couple of years after his return from Letterman and had pulled him out of some tough scrapes when his brothers weren't around to do it. Bill had moved to Long Beach California in nineteen fifty-five and was involved in sports for paraplegic athletes. He is legendary for pioneering Para-Olympic basketball and was instrumental in leading one of the first teams that competed internationally. Of course, Glenn was very proud of his buddy and knowing how fond Glenn was of his old friend; Harry and Rita had no reason to doubt Glenn when he told them he was going to see Bill Johnson.

Whether Glenn attempted to contact Bill or not is uncertain. What is clear is that at some point during the day Glenn got into a taxi and made his way to Gene's house. The two ended up drinking and partying into the night. According to Rita, Glenn brought some of his Dexedrine and Milltown to share with Gene along with a bottle of scotch. Rita said Gene's wife told her that the pair spent a good part of the night ruminating about women then Glenn somehow convinced Gene that he needed to take a road trip with him back to Montana. According to Thelma's daughter, Karen, Gene's wife was very young at the time and felt helpless to dissuade her husband from taking off with Glenn in their little Fiat.

Rita said that both Gene and Glenn were full of liquor and drugs by the time they left Gene's house and Gene should not have been driving, but the two were on a mission by that point. She said it wasn't long before Gene's driving caught the attention of a state trooper who turned on his siren and lights and began to pursue the pair in his patrol car. Glenn later told family members that he panicked after the police started their pursuit and told Gene to drive even faster so he would have enough time to throw his bootlegged pills out the window. When it became apparent that the cop was catching up to their vehicle, Glenn said he grabbed the steering wheel and made the car swerve dangerously. Glenn's damaged impulsive brain compelled him to react and the results couldn't have been more devastating.

After Glenn grabbed the steering wheel, Gene's car slammed into an LA overpass abutment on East Hollywood Way and Taylor. The impact propelled Gene through the roof of his car and killed him instantly. Glenn was thrown from the car and injured, but survived the accident. An ambulance picked him up and took him to St. Joseph's hospital where he remained for two weeks and then was transferred to Sepulveda VA Hospital.

Rita told me that Thelma and Skinny's hearts were broken beyond repair after Gene's death. Skinny would never allow Glenn near his family again and Karen said that even though her mother knew it wasn't really Glenn's fault; she stood by her husband and shunned Glenn. Karen indicated that she believed her mother suffered more than anyone else because she had not only lost a son but the little brother she loved so dearly.

Glenn's friend Bill Johnson

Glenn and Harry 1952

CHAPTER 14

Gay to the Rescue

Nor do born brothers judge, as good or ill,
their being.
From Born Brothers by Mark van Doren

After Glenn was released from Sepulveda, he travelled back to Missoula to live with his father once more. When he returned, Glenn discovered right away that Mom had remarried. Sources from Gay's family say that Glenn was inconsolable and furious. Among his ranting and ravings at the time were some credible threats toward Mom indicating that if he had to spend the rest of his life trying to find Mom, he would find her and break her neck.   Glenn also attempted to pester Grandma about our whereabouts but that sure didn't work for him. Grandma met him at the door with the business end of a mop and some very salty directives as my aunt called the police in the background. When the police arrived at Grandmas, they escorted a very irritated Glenn back to his Father's house and warned him not to go near my grandmother again.

Meanwhile, Gay's wife, Dusty, wrote to my mother and told her about Glenn's threats and behaviour. In her letter, Dusty expressed concern for Mom's safety as well as the safety of Myra and I.   My Grandmother also worried that Glenn would find us and told my mother about his visit. That's when my mother started warning us about talking to strangers, especially tall men with dark curly hair.

I've been told that Glenn spent some pretty lonely days in Missoula after his release from Sepulveda believing his family would never want anything to do with him again after Gene's death, but he was wrong. Glenn had been back in Missoula about a week when his brother Harry and young son Jimmy came to visit. Jimmy told me years later about how he and his father walked into the Oxford Club in downtown Missoula where Glenn was seated on a barstool at 10:30 in the morning with his bottle of beer, pack of cigarettes and a plate of half eaten eggs and bacon. Jimmy says that when Glenn looked over and saw them, he cried.

I was starting first grade at Bancroft Elementary School in Spokane Washington when Glenn voluntarily admitted himself to American Lake Hospital in September of nineteen sixty-one. He kept ruminating insanely about Mom and had a breakdown of sorts. David called Hugh and told him how Glenn was acting, so Hugh came and got him and took him to American Lake VA Hospital for treatment. Glenn spent a little over three months there, was released and then readmitted a month later. In April of nineteen sixty-two Dr. Malmstad contacted Hugh and told him that he recommended Glenn be permanently committed to the psychiatric facility at American Lake and that if they disagreed, he would not release Glenn unless someone in the family agreed to become his legal guardian. When I called American lake to see if they had any of Glenn's medical records, the only thing they had was a memo from Dr. Malmstad stating that Glenn was not to be admitted again without being fully committed to their psychiatric facility. Apparently they thought it was important enough to keep just in case Glenn ever made an appearance on their doorstep again.

Hugh told Gay, Harry and Thelma about the Doctor's recommendation. Of course Hugh, Harry and Thelma had seen firsthand what Glenn could do and was not about to expose their families to that again. Gay had been living in Helena Montana with his family and had not been around Glenn as much as the others, so he decided to be Glenn's guardian and take him to Helena to live with him and his family.

Gay, from all accounts, was the brother who felt as though he could handle anything and make anything work the way he wanted it to either by fist or fury. Gay was the oldest, shortest and toughest of all the brothers, and the impressive boxing skills he acquired in the U.S. navy assisted him in driving home his various talking points. Gay would never accept "can't or won't" and was even breaking horses at age sixty according to his daughter, Nancy. Gay's strong sense of familial duty always compelled him to come to the rescue of his other siblings whether they believed they needed it or not. Gay just wasn't about to let those doctors at American Lake lock his little brother away for good.

Gay picked Glenn up from American Lake in April of nineteen sixty-two and took him down to Helen to live with him and his family. Gay's children recall some pretty hair-raising times with their uncle Glenn. Gay and Dusty's daughter, Nancy, remembers Glenn holding a pistol just above her father's head as he lay passed out on the bed after a night of drinking. Nancy said Glenn was speaking directly to Gay and said, "I should do to you what they did to me." Nancy said that her mother heard the commotion from where she was in the living room and rushed in and wrestled the gun away Glenn before anybody got hurt. Of course, Glenn's physical condition had deteriorated considerably by then and he was drunk, so it was probably a lot easier for a small woman like Dusty Carter to get the gun away from him than it would have been otherwise.

Linda Carter also stated that the violent episodes Glenn created mainly occurred when he had been drinking, and was quick to point out that there were some good times when he was sober. She told a story about Glenn that illustrated that point. Linda said that one night Glenn came home from drinking and was hungry, so he grabbed an open can of tuna out of the refrigerator and ate it. The next morning, Dusty informed Glenn that the tuna he had eaten in the refrigerator was actually cat food that she had intended to feed to her

Siamese cats. The family had a laugh at Glenn's expense and Linda said Glenn didn't seem too upset about it. She said he did, however, attempt to get revenge by putting a dried-up cow pie in Dusty's Avon kit. Fortunately, Dusty discovered the cow pie before she made her rounds in the neighbourhood and put it somewhere Glenn couldn't find it. The next morning when Glenn woke up on the couch after a night of drinking; Linda said he was face down in a dried-up cow pie. I guess that continued until there was not enough left of the cow pie to make a good joke out of anymore.

Glenn enjoyed teasing and practical jokes so much that Gay not only referred to him the as eternal teenager, but also as the eternal juvenile delinquent. Most of the time Glenn's antics weren't as tame as the joke he played on Dusty, but were more childishly perverse. Unfortunately polite society is much more tolerant of misdeeds performed by a child who doesn't fully understand what they are doing as opposed to the childish deeds of a thirty-four year-old man with an evil sneer on his face. Glenn, however, was imprisoned within his own brain, which could not perceive what was appropriate and what was not.

One of the big worries Dusty had concerning Glenn was the safety of her children when he was having a seizure. Gay's daughters said they had witnessed Glenn convulsing on several occasions and described the seizures as ones in which his arms and legs would beat the ground violently, his mouth would foam and his hands would open and close like claws looking for something to grab. Nancy said the first time Glenn went into one of his convulsions after settling in at their house, Gay stepped over to see how he was and one of Glenn's hands clamped onto the back of his leg and wouldn't let go until the convulsion was over. I'm told that there was some skin peeled back on Gay's leg and it was black and blue for some time. Nancy also said when Glenn first started living there Dusty would help Glenn get into bed night after night when he got home after a night of drinking. After a while Nancy said her Mother got tired of it and just put a blanket over him wherever he decided to pass out.

Glenn lived with Gay in his family a little over two years before wearing his welcome out. The straw that broke the camel's back came with the revelation that Glenn had been abusing at least one of Gay and Dusty's children. Glenn, of course, denied the allegation, but Gay had at long last been convinced that something bad had transpired between Glenn and one of his children. After Glenn was confronted by his brother, he became furious and chased the child in question down the cellar stairs with a hammer. Fortunately, Gay anticipated Glenn's reaction and was right behind him tackling him to the floor before he could strike the child.

Gay moved his family back to Missoula in October of nineteen sixty-four and left Glenn behind in Helena. He rented a room for Glenn at the Park Hotel in downtown Helena then sent him an allowance each month for food and miscellaneous expenses. Gay was again faced with the choice of committing his little brother to a VA psychiatric ward or letting him live out his life free to go where he pleased. Even after all that had transpired, Gay just couldn't bring himself to commit his little brother.

Gay alerted Fort Harrison VA medical center about Glenn's situation and even made a trip there with Glenn so he would know how to find it. He also gave Glenn the information about the VA facility in Sheridan Wyoming which was bigger and had a lot more staff. By all accounts, Glenn seemed to prefer the Sheridan facility and spent more time there than he did at Fort Harrison when he felt particularly wound up. In November nineteen sixty-four, Glenn showed up at Fort Harrison and was described as being depressed and tense after a run-in with the police. He was quoted as saying, "I'm thinking about getting me a cop." Shortly after, Glenn requested a transfer to the Sheridan VA hospital, stating that he didn't trust himself to stay alone in his hotel room. His request was granted.

Glenn's statement about not feeling secure in his hotel room most probably had a lot to do with his ever eroding physical health and the increase in seizure activity he was experiencing. Whatever the reason, Glenn seemed to find solace in the V.A. hospital. The staff at the V.A. hospital made sure he took his medication regularly and was comfortable. In retrospect, it might have been the kindest act of all had Glenn's family taken Dr. Malmstead's advice and arranged for Glenn to be permanently committed to an appropriate V.A. psychiatric facility.

1963 Glenn in Helena

NAME	AGE	SEX	WARD NO.	CLAIM NO.	NAME OF HOSPITAL
CARTER, GLENN A.	34	M	0509?	C 16 905 593	VAC, Ft. Harrison, Mont.

DIAGNOSES (List and number in order of clinical importance all established diagnoses for which treatment was given. Place the letter "X" before the one diagnosis responsible for the major part of the patient's stay.)

ICDA CODE

X1. CHRONIC BRAIN SYNDROME ASSOCIATED WITH BRAIN TRAUMA.
2. GRAND MAL, SECONDARY TO NO. 1.

3/2.9
353.1

VA 10—1004 COMPLETED

Major diagnoses noted but not treated

NONE.

OPERATIONS PERFORMED IN THIS HOSPITAL, DURING CURRENT ADMISSION

DATE

NONE.

SUMMARY (Brief statement should include, if applicable, history, pertinent physical findings, course in hospital, treatment given, condition at discharge, date patient can resume pre-hospital activity, recommendations for follow-up treatment, medications furnished at discharge, and competency opinion)

THIS 34 YEAR OLD LABORER CAME TO THE HOSPITAL BECAUSE HE FELT QUITE DEPRESSED AND TENSE. HIS HISTORY DATES BACK TO 1950 WHEN HE SUSTAINED A GUNSHOT WOUND OF THE HEAD. METALLIC PLATE WAS INSERTED IN 1951. SINCE THE INJURY THE PATIENT HAS BEEN SUBJECT TO GRAND MAL SEIZURES WHICH ARE FAIRLY WELL CONTROLLED BY SODIUM DILANTIN AND PHENOBARBITAL 3 TIMES A DAY. HE DOES NOT TAKE THESE MEDICATIONS TOO REGULARLY, HOWEVER, IF HE MISSES HIS SLEEP OR DRINKS ALCOHOLIC BEVERAGES, SEIZURES MAY OCCUR. SEIZURE DID OCCUR ON NOVEMBER 4, 1964 WHEN THE PATIENT STAYED UP VERY LATE WATCHING ELECTION RETURNS. HE WAS PLACED IN JAIL AND SINCE THEN HAS BEEN QUITE DEPRESSED. HE STATES THAT HE WANTS TO GO TO THE VETERANS ADMINISTRATION HOSPITAL IN SHERIDAN BECAUSE HE DOESN'T TRUST HIMSELF TO STAY ALONE IN A PRIVATE HOTEL. HE FEELS ANGRY AND SAYS "I'VE GOT IDEAS ABOUT GETTING ME A COP", REFERRING TO THE POLICE OFFICER WHO ARRESTED HIM. THE PATIENT PREVIOUSLY HAS BEEN JUDGED MENTALLY INCOMPETENT AND THEN HAS A GUARDIAN. PHYSICAL EXAMINATION WAS ESSENTIALLY NORMAL EXCEPT FOR THE PRESENCE OF WELL HEALED SCARS ON THE HEAD. ROUTINE MEMOGRAM AND URINALYSIS WERE NORMAL. HOSPITAL COURSE WAS UNCOMPLICATED. THE PATIENT HAD NO SEIZURES WHILE ON PHENOBARBITAL 32 MG. Q.I.D. AND SODIUM DILANTIN 100 MG. T.I.D. PSYCHIATRIC TREATMENT APPEARS INDICATED. TRANSFER TO THE VETERANS ADMINISTRATION HOSPITAL IN SHERIDAN, WYOMING, IS BEING REQUESTED.

TRANSFERRED TO THE VETERANS ADMINISTRATION HOSPITAL IN SHERIDAN, WYOMING 12-2-64.

Record from Fort Harrison 1964

CHAPTER 15

Final Chapter

Sun has set, Shadows come,
Time has fled, Scouts must go to their beds
Always true to the promise that they made.

Taps, fourth verse

Glenn passed away in the early morning hours of May 24, nineteen sixty-five, five years to the day he and Gene slammed into that LA overpass abutment on East Hollywood Way and Taylor. This phenomenon of two people with significant connections to one another dying on the same day several years apart has happened twice in my family.It has made me wonder whether certain traumatic events get imprinted so deeply on us that our souls just gravitate toward the date of that event when it's time to leave this world. It's something I'm going to ask God about when I see him.

It makes me sad to think that Glenn died under the very circumstances he feared he might, alone in his hotel room. The coroner attributed Glenn's death to natural causes, but I have to wonder what was so natural about a man's death that began on a battlefield in Korea and ended fifteen years later with a massive seizure while he was alone in a broken down hotel room. Had I been able to offer a Eulogy I would have said that the real Glenn Allen Carter died in Korea (or Letterman Hospital) when he was twenty years old but his body didn't get the memo and forced him to navigate his way through his own private hell for fifteen years.

Gay was the only member of Glenn's family to attend his services. He might have done so because of his obligation as guardian, but I got the impression that he did so mainly because he loved his little brother and knew that he wasn't really responsible for the things he did. Glenn had indicated to Gay previously that there was a beautiful little VA cemetery just south of Billings that he would like to be laid to rest in, so Gay carried out his wishes and had him buried there with full military honours.

Nancy told me that the day after Glenn's service; a man approached Gay as he was packing up Glenn's belongings from his hotel room. The man told Gay that he had been out drinking with Glenn the night he passed away and explained that he had given his wedding band to Glenn to hold onto because he did not want a certain lady he was interested in to know he was married. As it turned out, Gay was given that wedding band by the coroner who found it on Glenn's body. Gay naturally assumed that it was Glenn's wedding band from when he and Mom tied the knot so many years before and placed it on Glenn's finger prior to burial. Gay didn't know that it wasn't Glenn's ring and he told the man that came looking for it that he wasn't about to dig up his brother because he was fooling around. It appears that Glenn was somehow able to execute one last practical joke.

In nineteen-eighty, I visited Glenn's grave for the first time in my life. The grave is white and indistinguishable from all the other white gravestones that fill the cemetery except for his name and rank, dates of his birth and death and the words medical corps. In Glenn's clinical records he states that he was a machine gun operator during his service in Korea so I have surmised that because he spent the bulk of his service career at Letterman Hospital, they might have thought he was either medical staff or just made that his designation because he spent so much of his active service time at a medical facility.

The national VA cemetery Glenn is buried in is called Custer National Cemetery and is near the border between Montana and Wyoming in south central Montana. After finding Glenn's grave, I decided to climb to the top of Last Stand Hill just above the VA cemetery and scan the landscape around me. I could see the slim easy flowing Little Bighorn River off in the distance and remember thinking that the sagebrush covered landscape I was looking at contrasted starkly with the lush green grass of the cemetery where Glenn lay. Last Stand Hill is owned by the Crow Agency, but well over a century ago; it was the backdrop for one of the most ferocious and infamous battles between native Indians tribes and the Seventh Calvary division led by George Armstrong Custer. I think it's very suitable that Glenn should be laid to rest in that particular cemetery given the great parallels between Custer and the Generals who conducted the Korean campaign. At the bottom of "last stand hill." a huge stone memorial marker engraved with Custer's name and the names of all the men who died in his regiment stands in remembrance. The battlefield is quiet and peaceful now and it's hard to believe anything as catastrophic as the massacre of two hundred sixty eight men ever occurred there.

In nineteen eighty-four, nineteen years after Glenn's death; I moved to Portland, Oregon and got married. I knew that Hugh Carter and his family lived just across the river in Vancouver, Washington so I invited them to my wedding and they accepted. The ceremony was performed at a very special little white church by Oaks Park in Portland. My husband and I said our vows in front of about forty guests and after we did that we turned around to face the audience. That is when I looked over to the pews on my right and saw Hugh and his family. I could see Hugh's wife, Janet, clearly but Hugh had his handkerchief out and was blowing his nose. After everyone started exiting the church, Hugh pulled my mother aside and with tears in his eyes, he told her about how much I reminded him of Glenn. Mom said that she had never seen any of the Carter boys cry before and was a little taken aback. I believe Hugh's tears that day were long in coming for his beloved little brother whom he probably wished could have been able to, in a kinder world, give his daughter away in marriage.

Glenn's story is a tragic testament to the expansive boundaries of human endurance. In a letter he wrote to my Mother from American Lake Hospital he states, "I just wish things would work out for us for the kid's sake, but I guess the good lord didn't want me to be around them." This particular line in his letter tugs at my heart because it clearly illustrates the depths of his suffering. His acts were monstrous but his tears were real. Glenn was a wounded warrior who fought and eventually died in service to his country. He was a hero but so were the members of his family who risked everything they held dear out of their love for him. I am grateful to Glenn for his service to our country. I am grateful that because of his service, I was able to access money through the War Orphan's Educational Assistance Act and find my true calling in higher education.   Most of all, I am grateful to have been given his story which helped me finally understand that his actions toward me were unintentional and not because I was somehow unlovable. I am grateful for peace with him at last.

Glenn's Tombstone in Little Big Horn Veteran's
Cemetery

Telegram received from PAC, Fort Harrison, Montana stated "CARTER, Glenn A.,
C-16 903 993 cause of death natural causes and autopsy not performed." Patient
expired 3-26-65.

Glen Carter Dies in Helena

HOSPITAL SUMMARY

Death Notice

2nd part of Letter to Mom from American Lake
Hospital

Glenn in military parade 1954 in front of the
University of Montana